Reinventing You

By Jaroslav and Sara Tusek

International Leadership Institute Publications

Florida and Prague

Sara D. Tusek, Executive Editor

International Leadership Institute Publications

PO Box 950-788, Lake Mary, FL 32795-0788

USA

www.ili.cc

Publication History:

First edition, 2019

ISBN: 978-0-9786337-7-6

Cover and text design: Noah Shepherd, NY, NY

Published by International Leadership Institute Publications:

Leaders to Follow. Jaroslav B. Tusek with Sara Tusek. International Leadership Institute Publications, Lake Mary, FL, 2018.

Prague for Beginners: Finding Myself in Prague. Sara Tusek. International Leadership Institute Publications, Lake Mary, FL, 2017.

21st Century Jobs. Jaroslav B. Tusek and Sara Tusek. International Leadership Institute Publications, Lake Mary, FL, 2009.

From Idea to Book in Five Steps. Sara Tusek. International Leadership Institute Publications, Lake Mary, FL, 2019.

Three Things You Can't Do in Prague. Jaroslav B. Tusek and Sara Tusek. Servant Leaders Press (an imprint of International Leadership Institute Publications), Ponte Vedra Beach, FL, 2006.

Your Career Passport. Jaroslav B. Tusek and Sara D. Shepherd (Tusek). International Leadership Institute Publications, Ponte Vedra Beach, FL, 2nd Edition, 1993.

Your Career Passport. Jaroslav B. Tusek and Sara D. Shepherd (Tusek). International Leadership Institute Publications, Sewanee, TN, 1st Edition, 1991.

Leaders to Follow, 1991-2012; *Business Briefs,* 1992-1997

Careers, 1987-2012; *Servant Leaders,* 2005-2012; *continuous conversion,* 2006-2012

ALOE: A Lesson on English, 2007-2012

Other publications:

East Tennessee Business Journal/Chattanooga Business Journal, contributing editors and columnists, 1993-2008.

College to First Job: Step by Step. Sara D. Shepherd (Tusek). The University of the South, Sewanee, TN, 1988.

Looking Ahead. Sara D. Shepherd (Tusek). The University of the South, Sewanee, TN, 1988.

Career Development Handbook. Sara D. Shepherd (Tusek). The University of the South, Sewanee, TN, 1987.

Designing Your Future. Jaroslav B. Tusek. St. Lawrence University, Canton, NY, 1985.

Career Development Kit for Future Leaders: An Introduction to Career Management. Jaroslav B. Tusek. American Management Association, Hamilton, NY, 1984.

Career Search Kit for International Students: A Handbook of Sources for the International Job Market. Jaroslav B. Tusek. New York Institute of Technology, New York, NY, 1983.

Job Search Kit for the 80s. Jaroslav B. Tusek. New York Institute of Technology, New York, NY, 1981.

Table of Contents

Preface: *What's new in the job-search game?*

Reinventing Your Future is our 10th book on career development. You will find that we have covered three key areas in taking charge of your career and your life:

1) Knowing *who you are*, what you can offer, and the role of your job in your overall satisfaction and fulfillment as a person;

2) Knowing how to find and use the most-up-to-date information on *where the jobs are* and how to get a job you can like and do best;

3) Knowing and using techniques and strategies as *you reinvent your future*, both professionally and personally.

How the job market looks now

We published our 9th job-search handbook, *21st Century Jobs,* in 2009 during what economists term the US Great Recession of 2007-2009. People were being laid off, fired, or simply let go through no fault of their own when their positions were terminated as the economy reacted to Wall Street machinations that changed the face of huge corporations. By October 2009, the US unemployment rate was 10%, according to the US Bureau of Labor Statistics, and most countries around the world were feeling the impact of the US Great Recession.

Yet in the midst of dire economic news, there was hope. Presidential candidate Barack Obama campaigned on hope, and *21ˢᵗ Century Jobs* reflected the confidence we felt that the future would be better than the present. We have been in the career development field since 1978 and have seen many low spots, but there is always a rebound. The US economy, we were sure, was strong enough to rebuild itself no matter what punches it took. Together, employers and employees could do whatever was needed to come back better and stronger than ever.

Ten years later, we find that our hope and optimism are, in some ways, justified. The Great Recession was followed by a recovery, but it has turned out to be a peculiar recovery. The US unemployment rate is very low (3.7% in December 2018, according to the US Bureau of Labor Statistics). From this point-of-view, there is a labor shortage. Some cities and states are using economic incentives (sign-on bonuses and the like) to find enough workers for jobs that are unfilled. You could say the US economy is booming.

But many of the jobs being created are not the solid, stable jobs of the 20th century, with a decent salary, reasonable benefits, a chance to save for retirement, and an implied understanding with the employer that your good work will be recognized in terms of keeping your job or getting promoted. In other words, your job security is, at the very least, questionable.

A longer-lasting result of the recession has become apparent. Not only did people lose their jobs, but employers found that they could ramp up their profits significantly by weakening or ignoring four pillars of the US labor market:

1. The expectation of earning a living wage in a full-time job;

2. Bargaining power by the employee that is somewhat balanced against employer power;

3. Retirement benefits, pensions, and comprehensive health insurance;

4. The support of labor unions to negotiate contracts that are to some degree fair and equitable; these contracts serve as models for non-union jobs.

Contingent employment

One solution for employers during the US Great Recession has become an accepted business model for maximizing profits: hiring people as needed into jobs that have no promise of security and have minimal, if any, benefits. "Contingent employment" is the new normal, a buzzword for a market of short-term jobs with no strings attached by the employer or the employee. These include consulting assignments, daily work on call, internships, fellowships, grant-funded positions, and month-by-month employment. Many people juggle two or three of these jobs to make ends meet, with unfortunate consequences that cut into their social, family, and leisure time.

Thriving on change: Reinventing Your Future

In the employment market of the 21st century, having a set of skills and expertise, along with up-to-date educational credentials, is just the beginning of finding a job you can like and do best. More than ever, it is your responsibility to take charge of your career. This can be frightening if you are unsure of what you have to offer and where you want to go, but it can be liberating if you develop your ability to maneuver the job market in ways that will leverage your past work experiences to create opportunities for yourself and the people in your circles of influence.

For more than four decades, we at International Leadership Institute have been dedicated to helping people find jobs they can like and do best. We've worked with thousands of people from dozens of different countries, with widely varying educational backgrounds, ages, skills, talents, job experiences, goals, and values. Some of the people we've worked with have built spectacular careers; others have more modest accomplishments but are no less satisfied with what they've chosen to do.

It takes courage and commitment to find a job you can like and do best. We can supply the know-how, but it's up to you to supply the personal energy, enthusiasm, and desire to learn and grow. If you do the work laid out for you in this book, you are well on your way to reinventing your future.

Acknowledgements

We have many people to thank for helping us bring this book to publication:

- Our clients in Europe and in Florida for the *Reinventing Your Future* career workshops: *Your Next Job*, *Looking Ahead*, and *Redirect*.

- Our student participants in the *American English Language Institute* programs, both in Prague and in Florida.

- Our consulting clients in educational organizations in Prague.

- Our career seminar clients, students, and program participants from St. Lawrence University, The University of the South, Covenant College, New York Institute of Technology, Seminole State College, and other American colleges and universities.

- Our executive and professional clients from the Career Group in New York City.

- Our young adult program participants from the American Management Association's *Operation Enterprise* programs in Canada, California, Florida, Virginia, and North Carolina.

- Our International Leadership Institute (ILI) program participants, both executives and students, from the Czech Republic, South Korea, China, Japan, Vietnam, France, Switzerland, Slovakia, Lithuania, Germany, Ukraine, Macedonia, Bulgaria, Croatia, Bosnia and Herzegovina, and Romania. These individuals took part in ILI programs delivered in the US and Europe: *Business Leadership Forum: USA, American English Language Institute, Travel-and-Learn,* and *Reinventing Your Future* programs.

- Our close friends, employers, colleagues, and family members with whom we've had deep and complex conversations about career development in general and their own careers. Some of these have been clients; others have acted as sounding boards; all are part of our personal and professional networks. We are more than grateful for all the encouragement, direction, Socratic questions, feedback, and laughter we have shared with each other. Truly, your career is not all about you, and you can't do it all by yourself.

Introduction: Take charge of your career

In this, our tenth book on the job search and your career, we have summarized for you what it takes to get a job that you will enjoy and in which you can excel. We offer up-to-date advice and strategies for job-seekers as well as enduring principles for taking charge of your career. If you invest sufficient time and energy into using this handbook, we are confident that you, the job-seeker, can equip yourself with all you need to win the game of finding, on your own terms, a job you can like and do best.

Why have we written *Reinventing Your Future?* Since 1970, when *What Color is Your Parachute* by John Bolles was first published, most career development practices were aimed at helping job-seekers to build a career by matching their personal talents, goals, and abilities to existing jobs in stable, well-defined industries.

The emphasis on understanding and defining yourself in order to explore careers and market yourself to potential employers was simple: there was, out there, a world of work that was rationally arranged and accessible. In it, industries were organized by function and rested on educational attainment and specific skillsets.

What's more, those industries seemed to be destined for continuous existence. Examples included education, healthcare, social services, business (manufacturing and finance being important sectors), entertainment, the law, journalism, architecture, and management. Anyone could research jobs by starting with an industry, identifying key companies/organizations, and then sifting through jobs in terms of requirements and responsibilities. The system, while not always fair, seemed to be logical and efficient. And you, with some hard work and imagination, could find a good match and become the productive and satisfied employee you wanted to be.

But all that has changed and keeps changing. This book covers the realities of the new "job market," one in which preparation for what already exists is not enough. We believe that if you, the reader, study this handbook, do the exercises, and develop faith in your own abilities, you will be able to navigate the emerging opportunities to find and keep a job you can like and do best even in the midst of continuing change and uncertainty in political, economic, environmental, and social realities all over the world.

Although the wide-open, chaotic, multi-cultural, and multi-lingual job market has become the new normal in every part of the world (replacing the old ways of getting a job based on education, social class, and having the right contacts), a few things have not changed. You are still in charge of how you think about yourself, where you find your energy, and which jobs you choose to pursue.

In the introduction to our 2009 book *21ˢᵗ Century Jobs*, we described what it takes to be in charge of your own career:

- Ability to identify and respond to needs which surround us (specifically, those needs we have chosen as priorities);

- Strong communication skills, especially across cultures;

- The ability to process and adjust to new information and situations;

- Resilience, both mental and physical;

- Willingness to accept responsibility;

- Patience to listen;

- Ability to inspire and involve oneself in team- and coalition-building;

- Wisdom and insight into people's motivations;

- Optimism and positive thinking.

Recent surveys indicate that employers expect that jobseekers will be competent in the technical and professional skills needed for their jobs. This is the basic level of qualifications for any job. But beyond the basics are some skills that you will need to develop if you want to stand above other job candidates. Problem-solving, critical thinking, and writing clearly—these skills are all related and are the skills most valued by employers. We would add that analytical skills are also crucial: making analogies, being able to extract essential information, and see how one thing is connected to something that appears to be entirely different. These skills, involving objective analysis, evaluation, and deciding on a course of action, are used every day in every kind of work setting.

So no matter how much we think we are under the power of social media, international trade policies, the high cost of education, the limitations of who we know, the responsibilities we have to our families, friends, and communities, and all the other circumstances that seem to constrain us, we are still in charge of what really counts: our own confidence in ourselves and our ability to move our lives in the directions that we choose.

The confidence that we can adapt and thrive is greatly enhanced when we surround ourselves with people who share our enthusiasm for change and growth. These people become part of our most valuable career network, helping us find hidden job opportunities so that we can reinvent our future. In turn, we assist our network members in creating their careers. This is the way to not only reinvent your future but also make a positive difference in your community and the world. We invite you to begin the exciting process of taking charge of your career!

Chapter One: You are in charge of your career

Clearly, the future belongs to those individuals who fully understand the importance of being in charge of their careers. These people are imaginative, well-prepared, energetic, and well-educated. What's more, they demonstrate their communication, organizational, team-building, and leadership skills while acting on a simple idea: the importance of knowing how you want to influence the world. In a rapidly-changing global economy, *job security* in structured and highly-organized economic environments is giving way to *job ownership* that puts each person in charge of finding and maintaining employment in which he or she can excel.

The people who own the future understand why and what they should do with their lives. They assume that soon they will find golden opportunities leading to their particular destiny and that what they do in response to these emerging opportunities determines the degree of their success. These individuals possess the deep and unshakeable knowledge that they are in charge of their own lives and their own careers. No one else can be ready for the changes and opportunities in their careers; no one else can make the right decisions that will lead them to success. We want to help you fully understand the crucial importance of owning and constantly reinventing your future.

What does it mean to be in charge of your career?

Above all, being in charge requires confident knowledge and thorough understanding of your own capabilities, accomplishments, personal vision, and lifelong goals. This confidence and understanding are then communicated in all your interactions with the people in your personal and professional network, including potential employers, strategic partners, and investors in your own entrepreneurial endeavors. Being seen as capable reinforces your own self-image for being resourceful, innovative, and able to find opportunity in every seeming setback that comes your way. Instead of being discouraged by what you cannot yet do, you can be energized to take on and master every new challenge that comes your way.

Second, being in charge requires that you benefit from the highly-motivating awareness of all your career assets: your skills, abilities, competencies, qualifications, and experiences, as well as your creativity, intelligence, ingenuity, crazy ideas, and dreams. You know how you have used these assets in the past, and you can see how to use them in the future. You are ready to recognize opportunities and benefit from them in your career.

Third, all this focus on your own career needs to be balanced with the right attitude: humility that comes from understanding that you can't do this alone. You are part of a number of networks: people with whom you've worked, studied, socialized, worshipped, played sports, eaten a good meal, and shared a place to live. These people play an intimate part in your success, and you play the same part in theirs. The realization that you have received hard-won wisdom, knowledge, and caring from many people will, if you are truly interested in being in charge of your career, spark a desire to not just further your own success but bring like-minded people along with you in the process, helping them to succeed as well.

Throughout this book, we will dwell on your motivation to take charge of your career. We hope to inspire you to become fully aware of the two faces of your participation in the labor market: why employers need you, and what you want to gain from your career.

Why employers need you more than ever

We all can see that the world economy is not a calm lagoon but rather a turbulent sea. Most employers, regardless of their industry, geographic location, relative success and stability, and quality of leadership, are looking in every direction for help in keeping their organizations afloat in the face of global competition, rising costs, and ever-diminishing resources. All organizations must cope with the expensive necessity to replace workers as they leave the firm and to train and retrain all workers in the firm. Products and services change in response to the interests, needs, discretionary funds, and expectations of their customers, suppliers, marketing team, and board of directors.

What employers are looking for is a champion—someone to come into their lives and solve their most pressing problems. It may be unrealistic to expect that job candidates will be champions; after all, they rarely know the actual concerns of the firm where they are interviewing. But being unrealistic does not stop employers from searching for someone who speaks their language and can offer fresh ideas and pointed insights as to how to make the organization more profitable, more influential, and in better shape all around.

The good news is that you can be that candidate, and we can show you how to do so. Although the world of work is in a constant state of flux, some of your tasks as a job seeker/entrepreneur do not change. These are the tasks that you need to complete in order to be the best candidate and get the most favorable offer for the job you have targeted as one you can like and do best. Here's what it takes to become a champion:

1. Completing an honest and thorough self-analysis of your major accomplishments, skills, abilities, values, and career goals;

2. Evaluating which of your skills and qualifications are transferable to the new assignment, job, or career change you are contemplating;

3. Learning to write and use effective resumes and cover letters that highlight your strengths and make it clear that you can significantly contribute to the organization you are applying to because you are aware of the organization's mission, purpose, and culture;

4. Preparing for interviews by envisioning yourself in a particular job and articulating ways in which you can and will perform with excellence in that job;

5. Offering yourself as the candidate whose personal skills, experiences, interests, and potential are in harmony with the culture of the organization: its mission, purpose, and immediate goals;

6. Continually reevaluating all the steps above and modifying them in response to new opportunities.

None of these tasks are so difficult that you can't do them well. By thoroughly preparing for interviews (formal and informal), you will do a favor not only to yourself but also to the people who are interviewing you. You will make every minute of your interview productive, and you will make it clear that you have the energy, determination, courage, and commitment to succeed in your new position. This kind of imagination and creativity shows, rather than simply tells as a resume does, what you have to offer.

Naturally, all of this preparation serves several functions. You can insure that your interview will showcase the most relevant of your qualifications for the job in question. But, just as importantly, you can analyze the organization and the position in terms of your own overall career goals. It's as crucial that the organization fits you as that you fit the organization. Knowing how you can make a meaningful contribution to the firm not only gives you confidence in the interview process; knowing that the firm is a reasonably good match for your values, beliefs, and principles allows you to throw yourself whole-heartedly into the entire process.

It's not just about your work

If there is one critical point that this book is making, it's that you are completely in charge of your own life. It may not seem that way, especially if you are accustomed to seeing yourself as a pawn who is pushed around by circumstances or fate. Maybe you feel that you lack the education, social status, mental abilities, finances, physical strength, friends, experience, or ability to run your own life. You may see yourself as lacking the autonomy or personal power to do what you really want to do. More likely, you have never taken the time and space to delve into your own character enough to be able to define who you are, what you believe to be true, and how you want to be part of the community of humanity by making an important contribution to its development.

Work is just one aspect of your life, but it's disproportionately important. You spend maybe 1/3 of your hours at work; the money you make has to provide for your needs and the needs of people who depend on you. Much of your self-worth may be tied to your job, and your social status is certainly in part a function of where you work and what you do. Taking charge of your career, it appears, is crucial to taking charge of your life.

We believe that you have to ultimately take full responsibility for the quality of your life including the time you spend in the workforce. This book is most concerned with your career, so we will emphasize job-search strategies and techniques, but bear in mind that success in one area of life often leads to success in areas that may seem quite distinct. Applying these analytical tools to decisions in personal life will bring good results.

We will show you step-by-step how to organize your career so that you will gain the knowledge, skills, and attitudes needed for your most important tasks:

- Understanding of who you are and what you want from life;

- Knowledge of what you can contribute and why your contribution is valuable;

- Ways to gain access to education that prepares your mind for your chosen career;

- Strategies for writing resumes and cover letters that clearly communicate your qualifications to potential employers and investors;

- Techniques that help you get to the heart of interviews and find common ground with the people with whom you are meeting;

- Attitudes that enable you to be a vibrant part of the social networks open to you through your job, your school, your spiritual life, your friends and neighbors, your family, and your nation;

- Confidence in your ability to adjust to new circumstances and make the most of change.

Additionally, we will show you how to make career development a vital, on-going process in which you continually scan the horizon for new ideas and prospects that will help you adjust to and benefit from all the massive changes in the world economy that are likely to take place in the very near future.

Fulfilling your destiny

We believe that humans are more than interchangeable workers, students, citizens, and world inhabitants. Sometimes it may seem that we are being pushed into slots, sorted into categories, and trimmed to fit certain positions, but there is more to life than squeezing ourselves into whatever our society thinks it needs at the moment.

We believe that each person is a unique creation who has been given particular abilities, interests, and possibilities for living. We also believe in destiny—that there is guidance that can lead people to fulfillment in all areas of life, including their careers. And we believe that each of us is presented with golden opportunities that can change our lives for the better.

As a result of our beliefs, we want to be sure not to overemphasize the more quantifiable characteristics of life. In spite of our certain knowledge that being in charge of your career is a necessity in today's world, we would like to make a suggestion. Rather than focusing all your mental and emotional energy on the worrying aspects of ongoing change in the economy and the labor market worldwide, we invite you for at least a few moments to take your eyes off external symbols of success and powers such as wealth, political and social status, the ability to control others, a desire for approval and attention, material possessions, professional and academic titles, and so on. Turn your eyes, please, toward opportunities to serve people in their areas of greatest need and your greatest competencies, interests, and qualifications. Looking for ways to serve, we have found again and again, helps us recognize the golden opportunities that are hidden from view when we only seek to serve ourselves rather than focusing on the common good.

The more severe the chaos, the more urgent the need. If you perceive that there are injustices, gaps, imbalances, and inequalities in the society around you, you may find the opportunities you are seeking. If you find all around you a lack of creativity, imagination, courage, and willingness to risk, you are simply identifying places where you can contribute your very best. There will always be a need for your time, talent, and energy: it's up to you to decide where that need is greatest.

It takes courage to act, especially in situations that are complex and ambiguous. But as you become more confident in your own character and abilities, you'll find it easier to take the initiative and not wait to be asked to do something new, better, and different. Louis Pasteur is quoted as saying that "Fortune favors the prepared mind." Our goal in this handbook is to show you how to prepare your mind for success in your career. To that end, we are providing encouragement and instruction in specific methods for both choosing a career direction and getting a job that you can like and do best.

. . . .

Steps to Reinventing Your Future

1. Albert Einstein said that imagination is more important than knowledge. As you begin to look at career opportunities, how can you apply his insight to your own career?

2. What does it mean to move from being passive (waiting for someone to tell you what to do) to being in charge of your career? Think about a time when you took the initiative and had a good outcome. Don't limit yourself to jobs; maybe you stepped up in a personal relationship, school situation, or community problem. Write a short paragraph about how you decided to act and what outcomes you encountered.

3. Why is it vital that you take charge of your career? What might happen if you simply wait for good things to come your way?

Chapter Two: Who am I? What am I good at?

Our social identity rests in how we see ourselves and how we are seen by others. If we are not careful, what we do with our time, money, and energy can become the main definition of who we are. This is a short-sighted approach to life, as the things we do every day are not always in line with our true dreams, ideas, and desires.

Aligning the inner and outer selves is a major goal of career development. Although you may not have, at the moment, a job in the field of your greatest interest, you can at least have a job that doesn't conflict with your core beliefs and values. Once these beliefs and values are catalogued, along with your sincere interests and preferred ways to spend time, you can start building the description of your ideal job. You may never find your perfect, flawless, ideal job, but knowing what you are looking for can help you recognize situations that will be a decent fit and a reasonable match between you and a job. It can also help you see the danger signals in a job that simply is not for you as it is too far from what you are seeking.

Spend time getting to know yourself: your career portfolio

The exercises in this chapter can help you build a picture of who you are apart from your job: your skills, interests, past accomplishments, values, beliefs and goals. This self-portrait is your greatest asset as you ponder your future and look for a job you can like and do best.

You can do the following exercises on your own, with a friend, or in a *Reinventing Your Future* workshop. Collect all these written materials in a folder. This is your career portfolio and will supply you with a wealth of information for every kind of job-search activity: looking for and/or creating jobs you can like and do best; preparing cover letters, resumes, and thank-you letters; evaluating job offers; and seeking new opportunities throughout your career.

#1: *Five key questions to ask yourself*

If it's true that we only live once, then it's important to take our lives seriously. Too often we get so caught up in what we're doing that we don't take time to make sure that we're spending our time in ways that harmonize with our values, skills, and major goals. This exercise will help you think about your life from various angles. Answer each question in a few sentences.

1. What makes you smile (activities, people, events, hobbies, projects, etc.)?

2. Who inspires you most (anyone you know or don't know—family, friends, authors, artists, leaders, etc.)? Which qualities inspire you in each person?

3. What are you naturally good at (skills, abilities, gifts, etc.)?

4. What activities make you lose track of time?

5. What do people typically ask you to help them with?

#2: *Where have I been happiest?*

The point of this exercise is to give you insights about the environment where you can thrive. Looking back at your life, where have you been most happy with your circumstances? Answer each question in two or three sentences.

1. Think of a particular place (maybe a house, cabin, or apartment) where you really enjoyed your life.

2. Describe this place in some detail—how it looks, where it is, how you happened to be there.

3. Note what you did on a daily basis in this place.

4. List the people, animals, and so on that lived with you or were frequent guests.

5. Try to say, in 20 words or less, what it was about this place that made you happy.

Now put all the answers together to make a short narrative about your happiest place. You can derive some of your values and goals from this description.

#3: *"What I believe and why" personal statement*

A *belief* is a construct of the mind that defines your attitude about something. For example, you could say "I believe in honesty." Your mental construct includes the attitude that being honest is good, and lying is wrong.

Beliefs influence your actions. It's crucial to your happiness to know exactly what you believe and to live by your beliefs. Your beliefs concerning what is important in life have a direct impact on your choices and actions; taking time to write your major beliefs will give you a clear mind when the time comes to make tough decisions.

It's worthwhile to invest thought as to what you believe and why you hold certain values. You can imagine this as a personal manifesto or creed (from *credo*, Latin for "I believe"), a written statement of your guiding principles in life. The length is important: you'll need 2—3 pages to develop your creed sufficiently. Don't be afraid to be very honest—this is for you, and honesty will help you set your goals. *Note:* You can find an example in the Appendix.

#4: *Write your own obituary*

While it may seem odd to write an obituary for yourself, this exercise will help you see your life as a total package. Begin this exercise by imagining that your life is over. It's been long and productive, full of personal and professional activities. Now it's time for someone to write your obituary, summarizing the key events of your life. You can think of your obituary as a "life-goals-in-reverse" document that highlights the people, organizations, places, and happenings that have made up your time on Earth. Try to make your own obituary at least a page long, so you include sufficient detail to complete a portrait of your life's potential. *Note:* You can find an example in the Appendix.

#5: *My ten most successful accomplishments*

Before you can find your place in the world of work, you need to have a basic knowledge of what you have to offer. If you've been in the job market for some time, you can look at your past jobs and analyze your accomplishments so far. If you're just entering the job market or doing a reevaluation of your life, you can broaden your definition of "success" to include areas not typically labeled as work. In this exercise, you will write about your ten most successful accomplishments in personal life, academics, family, spiritual, athletics, and volunteer activities. Note that accomplishments, by definition, involve things you actively do, not honors bestowed on you.

What is an accomplishment?

Think of times you were completely happy to be doing what you were doing, and your attention was focused on accomplishing a specific task or project. When you completed the project, you felt pleased and satisfied. Think of ten accomplishments, and you're ready to begin. Below you'll find an easy way to organize each accomplishment. You will write ten of these descriptions, one for each accomplishment.

1. "As a . . ." Using this phrase helps you describe the complete situation around the event: why you were involved (as a 1st year law student, as a bank loan officer), who was there, where it happened, the time of year—anything that contributed to your enjoyment or sense of purpose. This should be one or two paragraphs long. For example, your first sentence might read as follows: *As Director in a non-profit organization, collaborated with a team of six employees in a $1.5 million fundraising project.*

2. Explain what you did. Give enough detail using action verbs such as implemented, collaborated, directed, communicated, organized, introduced, and analyzed to convey exactly what you had to do to complete the task successfully. Again, a couple of paragraphs should be enough. For example, your first sentence might read as follows: *Developed and implemented a fundraising strategy for a group of newly-arrived refugees from Bosnia and Herzegovina.*

3. Sum up the outcomes of your accomplishments, as they apply to your career choices. The phrase "As a result" will help you list the changes that took place in the situation because of

what you did. How can this result influence your future career? Spend some time looking at your accomplishments from an outsider's point of view. One or two paragraphs will complete this accomplishment. For example, your first sentence might read as follows: *As a result, was able to significantly improve my cross-cultural communication skills and gained valuable experience in teamwork, goal setting, and strategic planning.* Take your time writing these accomplishments. When you have them completed, read them aloud to a friend. Have your friend listen for any thread of continuing interests: maybe all your accomplishments center on starting new initiatives, solving technological problems, helping people in specific ways, or setting and attaining large goals for yourself. Be sure to write down these insights that will help you to identify your motivational patterns, your key abilities and interests, and your overreaching life goals.

Your ten most successful accomplishments form the basis of your career portfolio. In practical terms, your accomplishments are the core material for your resumes and interview preparation. In addition, if you read them carefully and ponder their meaning, you will find valuable clues and insights into what inspires you to give your best, both in professional and personal life.

Knowing yourself is a life-long process; the person you will become in a few decades may have quite different aspirations and competencies from the person you are today. Your professional experiences will change you in significant ways, so get into the habit of periodic self-evaluation (every year, perhaps) in order to rework your accomplishments as you see them in more depth and add new ones as you go along. Reinventing your future takes continuous observation and interpretation of your own potential, as revealed in your most important accomplishments.

#6: *My skills chart*

Draw a chart similar to the one illustrated here, using a software spreadsheet program if you prefer. Across the top list your ten accomplishments in abbreviated fashion, describing each in just a few words.

- ✓ Down the left side write the names of the skills you used in each accomplishment. You should have a minimum of 20 skills listed.

- ✓ Put an *X* in each box that represents a skill used in each accomplishment.

- ✓ Then add up each *X* to see which skills you use most frequently.

- ✓ Make a list of your 3 most-used skills. This is a handy reference when talking with employers about your strongest competencies in terms of a particular job.

Note: The skills listed here are merely a few examples. For many more skills, consult *What Color is Your Parachute* or a similar publication (see *Resources* for more details).

	#1	#2	#3	#4	#5	#6	#7	#8	#9	#10	TOTALS
Negotiating			X			X			X		3
Careful listening	X	X	X			X	X	X		X	7
Public speaking	X								X		2
Initiating				X				X			2
Managing	X			X				X	X		4
Organizing	X			X		X		X	X	X	6
Drawing						X		X			2
Designing	X			X		X		X		X	5
Publicizing	X									X	2
Working on a team	X			X		X	X	X		X	6
Directing	X										1
Evaluating	X				X		X	X			4
Writing					X		X				2

When you've completed this chart, note how often you've used a particular skill. For example, this person would list careful listening, organizing, and working with a team as her 3 most-used skills. This hierarchy of skills gives you a picture of what skills you can bring to a job and an indication of what skills you will look for in a job description. Naturally you may develop many more skills over time, but keep in mind that these skills are a good indication of what your favorite jobs may look like.

#7: *Self-Analysis of Values (Adapted from* Job Search Kit for the 80's *by Jaroslav B. Tusek)*

Imagine how these people and you would rate the importance of these values and accomplishments.

Use this scale: *3=very much; 2=somewhat; 1=not at all.* The highest totals reveal your most important values

Value/Accomplishment	My parents	My colleagues	My closest friend	Myself	TOTALS
A college education/grad school					
Success in academics					
Success in sports					
Good social life (popularity)					
Strong spiritual life					
Independence					
Prestige and respect from others					
Wealth					
Service in government					
Integrity					

Creative talent					
Open-mindedness					
Respect for others					
Taking risks					
Physical fitness					
Being law abiding					
Pleasure and fun					
Being outdoors					
Being of service to others					
Marriage and family					
Wisdom					

Your professional portfolio

When you have completed these seven exercises, you will have an accurate assessment (at least from your own perspective) of what you have done in the past that brought you satisfaction, a sense of accomplishment, pleasure, and inspiration. Print everything out and gather all these narratives and charts into a good-looking portfolio.

You will find that your portfolio is a personal treasure chest of information for career research, job-hunting, resume writing, interview preparation, and on-going evaluation of your career satisfaction. If you have given sufficient thought and attention to the exercises, your professional portfolio is an accurate reflection of your personal and professional life. It will grow as your career and life choices expand and develop. It's a good idea to review your portfolio yearly to gain new insights, compare your progress over the past few years, and see if there are areas of interest that you haven't yet explored.

Your portfolio can become a source of confidence that increases your understanding of what you can do well, especially when you are preparing for interviews or have just accepted a new job offer. Reviewing your accomplishments, skills, values, dreams, and goals will put you into a frame of mind in which you can easily discuss what you have to offer an employer.

Deep self-knowledge comes gradually and often through mistakes, failures, and seeming tragedies. You will never know all your own potential, but you can become familiar enough with your strengths and limitations that you can steer your career with dexterity and confidence. You will not only be able to spot golden opportunities but also create them out of the unmet needs you see in your present job, your industry, and the world. This is what it means to reinvent your future.

. . . .

Steps to Reinventing Your Future

1. Which of my skills do I most enjoy using? How can I incorporate them into a job?

1. Is it important to me to consider my values when I am at work?

2. Who decides how to evaluate and rank my accomplishments and contributions to my community?

3. How can I use the understanding and insights I am gaining as to my own beliefs, values, goals, skills, and accomplishments to reinvent my future?

Chapter Three: Doing your homework: career research and written communications

After completing your self-exploration in Chapter Two, it's time to do the other half of the job search: finding professional opportunities where you can thrive and make a meaningful contribution. Finding a job you like and can do best requires patient, in-depth research. Job-seekers in the 21st century have powerful tools to help them in this research, including the world-wide web, accessed through the Internet via your smartphone, tablet or laptop. Public and university libraries have basic reference books for career research along with free computers and the assistance of a librarian to find what you want efficiently. In fact, the problem for a 21st-century job seeker may be too much career-related information rather than too little.

Career research: the jobs that fits you best

Learning about jobs and the world of work begins when you are a child. Your family's social and educational background, expectations for you, and financial resources are a large determinant of your career. The people around you are role models who demonstrate what careers may be appropriate and desirable for you.

Education is expensive in the US. The majority of college graduates have some debt, with many owing tens of thousands of dollars. It is wise to calculate how much you can pay for your education before you go into debt. Consider the credentials needed for the career for which you are preparing vs. the prospects for jobs in that career field (look at projected demand, salary, geographic considerations, and so on). The *Occupational Outlook Handbook* (available for free online—see *Resources*) can answer many of these questions.

It's also wise to explore a career in person before you put time and money into preparing for it. Information interviews and job-shadowing experiences with people in that career field can be arranged through your personal or university networks. When you have your meeting, ask those professionals all the hard questions about their job to get an idea of what the day-to-day reality of that particular line of work is really like. Likewise, a summer job, internship, or volunteer experience will give you more practical information about a job than any college class and will make your resume stand out from thousands of others.

Standard career research includes these aspects of a job and organization:

- education requirements for entry-level jobs and for advancement;

- salary ranges at various levels of responsibility;

- typical daily, monthly, and yearly tasks;

- necessary professional development activities, including certifications;

- career pathway within the organization;

- growth potential of the organization in relation to its industry;

- general career outlook.for the industry and job, including international expansion and competition, effect of government regulations, and projected need for employees.

You can start with a job field or industry (for example, technology, fine arts, or the environment) and look for jobs within the industry. The *Occupational Outlook Handbook* and other industrial and professional directories can help you do your research. You can find valuable information on the Internet by accessing Federal government job-related websites using an "advanced search" web browser setting to limit your search to websites in the .gov domain so that you can pinpoint the most reliable government information on jobs and careers.

One thing to bear in mind is that within every industry, there is a wide range of jobs calling for quite different skills. For example, imagine that you want to work for your state government in "something environmental." If you have very good communication skills, your accomplishments seem to point you toward a job with constant interaction with other people, and you like to travel, you could consider a job where you represent the state as an Environmental Specialist, touring schools and libraries with environmental awareness programs. If you're an excellent writer, you could produce the Department of Environmental Conservation's magazine or write descriptions and press releases for state parks. If, instead, you like to read, gather information, and solve problems, environmental research is likely to be a job you'd enjoy.

And if your idea of environmental work is to get outside and get your hands dirty, then you could look into being a park ranger or working with a team of scientists examining the impact of humans on clean water. If you start with a list of your skills, interests, and values, theoretically you can find a job that might fit you in any industry.

Find a job that seems to fit you: the information interview

To begin this project, choose an industry or organization in which there are jobs that appeal to you. Do some solid research using several different kinds of resources so you get a balanced perspective. Directories of industries and jobs, respectable websites (.org or .gov), job listings from appropriate companies and institutions, and job boards all offer a wealth of information. You want to get an accurate and up-to-date picture of key aspects of the job, including the following:

- Level of education needed to enter the industry or organization, as well as the advancement process;

- Typical skills needed for both entry-level and middle-management positions;

- Daily functions and responsibilities;

- Geographical limitations, if any;

- Salary range for entry-level jobs; salary range for high-end jobs;

- Prospects for the job—how many new hires are predicted to be needed over the next ten years?

- Any hazards or problems associated with the job; any unusual problems in finding or keeping the job.

Find someone who has this job or one like it. Use your personal network of friends and family, your university's Alumni network, your spiritual or civic organization's membership, relevant professional directories, and business or organizational websites in that industry to locate a person who seems approachable. Get in touch with this person to set up an information interview—not a job interview, but a friendly conversation about the kinds of jobs you are exploring.

Formal job-shadowing experiences may be organized by university career offices or professional organizations. Generally, you will be assigned a department or a particular person to shadow for a few days at work. If you prefer to take a more informal route, you can ask around your networks to locate someone willing to have you observe the organization's routine for a day or two.

Information interviews and job-shadowing both offer a low-stakes, low-commitment way to see what an employee in that job or industry does every day. These are crucial exercises for getting real-life facts about a job before you make any commitments of time, money, and education.

Ethical concerns for your career

Every career brings with it ethical questions and choices. It's crucial to have a clear idea of your own ethics to help you find a good fit for a career and a specific job. Here are four questions for you to consider concerning your personal ethics and how you live them out at work.

1. *Have you ever made a big mistake at work?* Maybe you trusted someone with confidential information and regretted the outcome, or you cheated or prevaricated in some way, avoiding taking the blame for a bad decision. Write about one mistake in some detail:

   - What was the point of pain for you?

   - How did you deal with the pain?

   - What did you learn?

2. *Are there parts of your job or career field that make you anxious or uncomfortable?*

   - Why do you have this reaction?

- How can you manage your job to avoid these situations, or are they just part of the day's work?

3. *Have you ever covered for a colleague when he/she made a bad mistake?*

    - What do you owe your colleagues and your employer in terms of loyalty?

    - Is it ever okay to withhold or modify the truth?

    - Is peer pressure ever a good thing? Can it be a way to keep an organization afloat and avoid scandal?

4. *Is there such a thing as a career field or organization where everyone operates with complete transparency?*

    - Would you like to work in such a field or organization?

    - Are you willing to let your employer, customers, and colleagues see all your faults, if it is necessary for the good of the organization?

5. *Does your current job/career field match your ethics well?* Why or why not?

6. *Are there places you would never work or jobs you would never do?*

    - What are they?

- Why would working in them be unacceptable to you?

Volunteer work, community service, internships, and summer jobs

There are several highly-effective, hands-on ways of researching careers and building your professional network of contacts whether you're a student entering the workforce or a career changer seeking a new type of work.

Volunteer work and community service

These activities involve working as a productive member of an organization without being paid. Ideally, you take on specific tasks and are evaluated by a supervisor. Volunteer and community service activities include local help such as working in a hospital or church, doing chores such as lawn-mowing or home fix-up for the elderly, or tutoring at-risk children. Community service, a type of volunteer work, is a requirement at many businesses, professional firms, colleges, and universities; any of the volunteer activities mentioned can be used for community service experience.

Adventurous service projects stretch your boundaries; possibilities are helping to rebuild a hospital destroyed by a hurricane or establishing business networks in a country with few economic resources. Environmental groups offer volunteer vacations during which you can conduct research or measure key criteria in environmental change. Universities, churches, and other non-profit organizations sponsor volunteer exchange programs, many of which are country-to-country, giving you the chance to live abroad and develop your language and communication skills. The list of volunteer opportunities is limited only by your imagination. All these experiences give you a chance to explore careers of interest and develop job-related skills, giving you a personal perspective on the career you are exploring. The books on volunteering that are detailed in *Resources* can get you started.

Internships and summer jobs:

An internship or summer job is a working/learning experience in which you act as a responsible employee in an organization. Remuneration (money you are paid) may be none, a token sum, minimum wage, or a percentage of a first-year salary. Many businesses and organizations have formal internship programs for students and career changers or hire relatively inexperienced people for short-term summer jobs. On-line social media, TV broadcast studios, banks, insurance companies, manufacturers, government agencies, and scientific laboratories all offer internships and summer jobs to people who want to get their feet wet in a particular job or organization. An internship can give you as much information and skill development as a college course for free (or even for pay). Summer jobs may offer many of the same opportunities as internships or may be more clerical, depending on the organization. Most summer jobs are paid, though usually at minimum wage.

The best internships and summer jobs carry real responsibilities and are evaluated periodically by a supervisor. An internship can give you real-life experience in a career of interest as well as expanding your network of contacts and giving you some excellent job credentials in the form of letters of recommendation. There are extensive listings of internships on many professional, business, and college websites. The *Resources* section has suggestions to help you research internships.

Notes about written communications; cover letters, resumes, and thank-you letters

In this section, we offer strategies, advice, and techniques on how to make your written communications powerful and effective so that you get interviews and job offers. We purposely do not include samples of written communications because some participants in our programs tend to copy them almost word for word. It's to your benefit to start from scratch with writing your resume so that you can design it to highlight your most important job qualifications.

What we have found is that in order to most effectively develop these written job-search tools, you'll need an up-to-date career portfolio of your major accomplishments, your job-related skills, and your career goals. Presumably, you have such a summary; if not, the previous chapters of this book will help you create it.

It will benefit you greatly to write highly-individualized documents in which you manifest your personal talents, qualifications, interests and characteristics. Such a writing task is superb interview preparation: all the hard work of matching your skills and experience to a job is already done and thoroughly digested when you walk into the interview.

Cover letters

Every communication with a potential employer, even for an internship or summer job, should be accompanied by a cover letter. This includes emailed applications unless the employer specifically asks you not to send a cover letter.

Essentially, a cover letter introduces you as a job candidate and makes a short sales pitch for an interview. Remember, you are not trying to get a job offer yet, as you haven't even met the employer. You simply want a chance to talk about the ways you could help the organization meet its goals in the job being filled.

The cover letter will usually be read before the resume, so it needs to include the reasons why you are interested in the organization, your major qualifications, and how to get in touch with you. In fact, if your cover letter is poorly done, the chances are good that your resume will not be read at all. Many examples of basic cover letters are available on-line or at college career offices, whose services are often available to alumni as well as current students.

Cover letters use a business letter format. They must have no spelling or grammatical errors, so ask someone to read your letter before you send it. Use a high-quality paper for the letter, the resume, and the envelope when you are sending hard copies. For cover letters sent online, be sure the formatting will be correct if the letter is printed. Saving your letter in a PDF format will insure that it downloads and prints properly.

The content of the cover letter should make clear what kind of job you are looking for or the specific opening if you are responding to an ad. Include how you learned about the organization and what, on the basis of your research, attracts you to it. The cover letter gives you an opportunity to stress your specific qualifications that are relevant to the position for which you are applying. These qualifications should match the ones that are evidently important to your potential employer, as indicated in the ad or in the organization's mission statement (usually available on their website).

When you write the cover letter and resume, try to find or infer the keywords for the job. Keywords are usually found in the job description. They may be specific industry jargon (like Java for computer programming) or skill sets (like financial accounting or translation from French to Dutch). Often, big organizations have software programs that search for keywords in the documents you upload; if you omit the keywords, you are out right away.

Don't forget that the primary reason to write a cover letter is to get an interview. If you can get an interview some other way (through a personal contact or at a professional function) then by all means skip the cover letter, as it benefits the employer much more than you. Since you don't know everything about the job or position in question, you can easily include information that makes it simple to screen you out.

Resumes

Over the years, we have found that many job-seekers come to us because they want us to write their resume for them, thinking that it's a mechanical chore that can be done by filling in the blanks, like a job application form. Certainly, it's true that you can upload a resume format from the Internet and insert some facts about your education and employment background, but you are cutting yourself off from potential interviews when you take that approach.

We urge you to forget the idea of writing a "one-size-fits-all" resume and keeping it on file for every occasion. Although some career books focus on explaining how to write your resume as if it were a one-time chore, and some career agencies make their living by guiding you through writing a generalized resume, it would be most unhelpful to you to assume that the resume you have produced by these means is the best choice for all job searches.

What works best is to write a targeted resume for each job as you apply for it. You will of course need standard resume-type information regarding your education and previous employment; this material should be in your career portfolio. Your address, phone number, and email are included in this standard information. Keep all this information handy for the final draft of the resume. In the meantime, delve into the heart of the resume—the most relevant skills and experience you can bring to the employer for the job in question.

Targeting your resume

Employers are looking for potential as proven by initiative, competence, dedication, persistence, and outstanding communication skills. Interviewers are typically looking for evidence of these basic professional skill clusters:

- problem-solving skills (creative ways to envision and solve problems);

- computer literacy;

- quantitative skills (financial, budgeting, and simple accounting);

- management skills (organization, planning, coordination, teamwork, motivation, effectiveness, and the ability to do things the right way);

- fluency in foreign languages;

- listening skills and the ability to discern other people's point-of-view (empathy);

- job-related human relations skills (the ability to supervise and be supervised);

- proven leadership abilities.

Competency in technical and professional skills is taken for granted in professional fields such as engineering, computer science, architecture, interior design, communications, financial accounting, media, medicine, law, etc. Your educational attainments prove that you have the basic training and practical skills needed in your industry; the rest of your resume proves that you can use these skills effectively in real-life settings.

Different jobs put different emphasis on skills sets; therefore, it is important for you to know what skills are critical in the job you want so that you can slant your resume accordingly. If you are not sure about the skills needed in the job you seek, find out. The Internet provides unlimited information on a huge range of careers on websites run by the Federal government, state and city governments, and professional associations. Graduate school program descriptions can also provide a vocabulary and network of contacts for both career research and interview preparation.

To write a powerful and effective resume, you must be able to show how your skills, abilities, experience, and knowledge match the requirements of the job you seek. As you begin to create your targeted resume, you will need all the information you can find about the job you've chosen, starting with the basic competencies required and going on to the keywords that a software program uses to screen your resume in or out.

You need to know who can actually hire you for the job; often Human Resources screens applicants but does not hire anyone directly. Find as many details as you can glean about the actual working conditions and the hiring timelines. Much of this information may be found in a job listing, but most listings conceal as much as they reveal, and you may be working with very little concrete information.

Once you know the skills and criteria for the job you want, the next step is to illustrate what qualifications and experiences in your background best document these required skills. Refer to your career portfolio from Chapter Two and begin to gather facts about yourself illustrated by your experiences in previous jobs, college or graduate course work, hobbies and extracurricular activities, professional or student organizations, volunteer work, internships, field work assignments, summer jobs, professional associations, etc. These facts will form the body of your resume and will demonstrate your abilities to be competent and effective in the kinds of assignments that interest you, as well as your potential for what you can do in the future.

Your resume communicates who you are and what you can do

Your resume is the professional "you" on paper. Frequently, it is the first picture of you and your capabilities that a potential employer will see. The resume must illustrate your potential as it pertains to the job in question. What you have achieved and accomplished in the past is the only indication the employer has of what you will do in the future; therefore, your resume must accurately illustrate what you have accomplished, in school or in work settings. It should be

- concise, (preferably one page only, unless it's an academic Curriculum Vitae/CV which can run to 50 pages or more, listing every publication, conference, panel presentation, seminar, and other aspect of academic life);

- logically ordered;

- easily read, with no typos or spelling errors.

The key to an effective resume is clear, simple, concise language with a focus on your most relevant skills and accomplishments. You need to communicate that you are an exceptionally well-qualified candidate who has fresh ideas and a strong grasp of what is needed in the job you are applying for. Be sure that every word in the resume brings the employer or interviewer back to your one goal: to get an interview.

Poorly-thought-out resumes are typically only a general record of dry, rather impersonal facts about a job seeker; they may contain as many reasons why a certain employer might not be interested as otherwise. Leave out unimportant information. Condense, trim, delete, and clarify. Employers have very limited time to read resumes, and you should endeavor to help them in this regard. The most pertinent facts and skills should stand out at a glance and not be buried in verbose, murky, unclear descriptions.

Stress results achieved by giving concrete examples of what you accomplished. Be sure to use action-oriented verbs to describe your accomplishments. For dynamic impact, start with action words such as implemented, oversaw, organized, completed, increased, initiated, delivered, and evaluated. Don't use the same word twice in one paragraph unless you have a reason for emphasizing it.

Sentences or phrases should be short, ten words maximum, beginning with a capital letter. Leave out the personal pronoun *I* and the articles *a* and *the*. Avoid weak, overused phrases such as *was responsible for, duties included, assisted in,* and *worked on.* You are not writing a job description. Focus on action--what you did rather than what you were. Quantify (use numbers or percentages) whenever possible: number of people, number of items, amount of money involved, amount of time saved. Use numerals, not words (*10*, not *ten*). If you are changing careers into a new industry, it helps to use the vocabulary (especially the keywords) of that industry to describe your experience. Learn this vocabulary from company literature and job descriptions.

Write and rewrite your experiences, trimming your wording until it projects, in as few words as possible, the sharp, clear image of you as an achiever. Review it with others and with your career counselor, if you have one.

Resume formats

The resume does not have to be chronological; often a mere chronological outline of your past experience becomes your "obituary," as it makes you appear unqualified for the job in question by what it highlights and what it omits. An effective resume should focus on those skills, qualifications, and experiences which the employer is seeking. Your task is to communicate your outstanding qualifications for the position in question.

Up until now we have been placing the emphasis on substance and content as represented by your life's experiences rather than on arrangement or form. But in the case of written communications, neatness does count. Be careful about correct formatting, grammar, and spelling; your resume will often be your only representative. Be sure its appearance matches the fine qualifications it presents.

Accompany your resume with a cover letter. Wherever possible, address correspondence in the name of an appropriate individual in the organization to which you are applying. Consult the organization's website or someone you know who works there for this information.

Although there is no one right way to arrange the text of your resume, there are some generally recognized approaches. Each of these has its advantages and disadvantages. You can choose one format, combine two or more, or invent your own. Take into account the expectations of the employer, any constraints that may be presented if you are uploading a resume (sometimes the file format and character count are specified), and the relative appropriateness of one approach over another in terms of your qualifications.

#1: Letter of application as a substitute for resume

This letter format is particularly appropriate in applying for a specific position which you have selected as the right possibility for you and is an especially useful tool in answering help-wanted ads. Here we suggest you study the ad carefully and try to come to some understanding of the essence of the advertised job. Open your letter reflecting this. Here's an idea for the opening: "I noticed in (the newspaper, a website, a job board) your advertisement for a person who will . . ."

After a thorough examination of the ad, pick out of your inventory of qualifications those items which best demonstrate your abilities pertaining to the advertised position. Be sure to use the language of the ad and try to include relevant keywords and phrases. You may also consult the organization's website for more wording that reflects their stated values, goals, and mission. Unlike the customary resume, this type of letter will say nothing that is not pertinent to the job the employer is seeking to fill. A word of caution: don't forget to ask for an interview!

#2: Functional (skills-based) resume

The content is arranged under headings which are intended to describe your capabilities (skills sets): Research, Design, Customer Relations, Supervisory Experience, Sales and Marketing, and so on. Under these headings, details are provided from past activities. This approach is especially appropriate for the recent college graduate without much work experience related to his or her chosen field or for someone changing careers to a fairly closely-related field.

#3: Chronological resume

The chronological resume presents the facts about you in reverse chronological order with the latest experiences given first. This form is distinctly problematic for the job-seeker with little or no relevant experience or for those with gaping holes in their career chronology, such as time taken out for child-rearing, starting your own business, extensive travel, and so forth. Yet often employers prefer the chronological resume, either for its reassuring familiarity or its outright simplicity. It's most suitable for people with a successful track record and plenty of experience in their chosen career filed.

$4: Combination resume

This resume, as the name implies, is a hybrid of the above two types. It may start with a qualifications summary that stresses functions (skills and abilities rather than experience), then move on to a brief chronological overview.

#5: Qualification brief

This type of resume stresses the fact that you are uniquely qualified for the position you are applying for. It will above all focus on your qualifications, rather than providing historical information about positions and jobs you held. If done well, it is far more powerful than a regular resume as it contains only the information that will make an employer want to interview you immediately. Bear in mind that, as the title suggests, this is a brief communication.

Thank-you letter (sent immediately after the interview)

This letter reminds the interviewer about you and your qualifications for the job. It gives you a chance to call attention to the strong points of your application, to reaffirm your interest in the organization, to briefly recapitulate your strengths for the job, or to add pertinent qualifications to your application which you may have not presented previously. However, be sure to pick only those points which are most relevant, and keep it brief. In your job search, the thank-you letter gives you a golden opportunity to do five things:

- Thank each person with whom you spoke;

- Build on an area of mutual interest;

- Repeat your strong interest in working for the organization;

- Offer additional information;

- Politely remind the interviewer about any indications he or she made as to when you'll hear about the next steps in the interview process.

Follow-up letter

This is to be used to call further attention to your job candidacy after waiting a reasonable length of time without response to your initial application. Here you need to be tactful, not appearing to reprimand the employer for tardiness. Some of the same items suggested for the thank-you letter may be included in your follow-up letter. If you can add new, relevant qualifications that are particularly important to that organization, all the better.

Get help if you need it

Very few people can manage to write all these detailed, information-packed pieces of career and job-related communications without help. Even if you are a talented writer, most likely you are not familiar with the specific demands of writing cover letters, resumes, and follow-up letters. Rather than showcasing your style, vocabulary, or ability to make an argument, business communications have one purpose: to say just enough about you to make you stand out and get an interview without revealing your weak points and lack of experience.

You need to ask someone to look at your written communications with an objective eye. Have you presented your best professional self? Do the cover letter and resume show what a good match you are for the particular job in question? Have you avoided including information that is irrelevant or downright harmful to your job candidacy? It takes an outside eye to see all this.

Naturally, you must find and correct every typo, misspelling, incorrect punctuation, and vaguely-worded phrase. Your formatting must be done in such a way that an uploaded resume will print out correctly (PDFs work well for this). If your computer skills are haphazard, you may want to pay someone who has excellent skills in WORD or whatever software is accepted. And if maneuvering a website to answer questions about yourself and upload your documents is not your cup of tea, hire someone who knows how to do it.

If you are a university student or graduate, the Career Services office may help you for free or for a token fee. If you have friends who know how to do these things, buy them a nice meal and ask for help. Use every resource you can find at this stage of the game; researching and writing targeted resumes is the only way to stand out in the highly-competitive job market unless you have many friends in high places. All the effort you make will be repaid in terms of helping you do better next time, if you don't succeed right away, and you will be well-placed to reciprocate when the people who helped you are in need of your help in return.

. . . .

Steps to Reinventing Your Future

1. What are the disadvantages and possible problems of sending a resume to a potential employer?

2. What are keywords, and how can you use them to your advantage?

3. What is the relationship between your resume and an interview with someone in a position to hire you for a specific job?

4. Choose one of your ten most successful accomplishments. Now describe it in five sentences or fewer. Add one or two skills that you used in the accomplishment. This is your "three-minute elevator speech," which you should be able to produce on demand whenever you are in a situation to talk about your job qualifications on short notice or in an unexpected meeting.

Chapter Four: Getting job interviews--you are part of many networks

Networking, or "you know more people than you think!"

Effective networking rests on knowing and being interested in people and their lives. True networks consist of individuals with some common experiences, shared values, and knowledge of each other's abilities. Real, functional networks are made of people who care about each other, are willing to help others, and open to being helped in their lives. These networks are precious and should not be misused by careless people who are just looking for a job, with no intention of reciprocating the favors gained from the network. If used with generosity and common sense, your networks can open up the hidden job market for you—the jobs that are not advertised and are only known to a few key people in the organization. Some surveys estimate that 70% of professional jobs are only open through the hidden job market. They are not to be found in the public market of ads.

In the 21st century, networking is easier than ever. Instant communications around the world are taken for granted: Twitter, smartphones, Instagram, Snap Chat, Facebook, LinkedIn, and thousands of private social media networks make it easy to get in touch and stay in touch. Information exchange goes in all directions, from up to down to sideways and up again.

Practically speaking, the more people you know, the more jobs you will hear about, especially the great majority of jobs in the hidden job market which are never advertised publicly. The more people you know, the more likely it is that someone will recommend you for an interview. People like to interview people they know or who are recommended by someone they know for three solid reasons:

- If someone recommends you, you are probably socially acceptable.

- The interviewer can unofficially check out your character and abilities through personal conversations.

- There's a much greater likelihood of a job match as you've been prescreened.

Recognizing and organizing your network is a logical step in the job search. Just bear in mind that the people in your network don't exist merely for your own benefit. If you tap someone's contacts, you need to be careful not to burn them and hurt the original contact. Thank people for what they do for you; keep them informed as to your progress. In general, treat them like important people to whom you owe a debt of gratitude (which you do) and show them respect. Remember that networks run in many directions, so when someone in your network wants your help, give it freely and gracefully.

Job ads

Traditional job advertisements are still a viable way of connecting job seekers with opportunities in the open job market. These ads are found in online social media membership sites as well as in print or online in local or national newspapers, commercial job boards, professional journals, and digital bulletin boards. These ads typically give the necessary information about a job or refer you to the website of the employing organization for more details. These ads are attractive in that they appear to give you the opportunity to choose which job you're interested in, in much the same way that a restaurant menu lets you choose a meal. You get the feeling you are in charge! But you are not, as millions of other people can read the same ads and apply for the same jobs, creating such competition that you may never get an interview, let alone an offer.

Bear in mind these general rules about job ads:

- Some ads are legitimate. There is an actual opening, and the requirements listed will be used to screen applicants. Especially in the case of public institutions that receive government funding (schools and colleges; military bases; public hospitals; local, state and federal governments, for example), the employer is legally bound to advertise all openings. Jobs posted from these organizations are, more often than not, reliable openings.

- However, even though there may be an opening, often the ad is a formality in the sense that a strong internal candidate already exists. In many cases there has been an "acting" employee filling the job. His or her performance has been satisfactory, and the ad is simply a necessary compliance with government hiring practices that are meant to promote job equity and fairness. To you, this means that you may be very well-qualified for the job, but in reality, you have a very small chance of getting the offer. You may be asked to interview so as to leave a respectable record that the institution acted in accordance with the law in the interview process, but the internal candidate has many advantages over you, not the least of which is that he or she is already doing the job.

- Some ads are simply fake. They may be fraudulent (scams), especially if they ask for money from you. Sometimes employers place vague, generic ads to gather a pool of applicants that they can hold till they actually have an opening.

Knowing this, you can wisely use job ads when appropriate. You may be able to find jobs and apply for them online, which is easy and comfortable. But the chances of your job application resulting in a job you will like and do best are significantly smaller than looking for a job through personal contacts. Your contacts give you far more information about the reality of possible jobs; your contacts also get your application through the pre-screening process, increasing your ability to get interviews. And interviews are the key to finding a suitable job for you.

Getting Interviews

When scheduling interviews, you want to make your appointment with people who are high on the chain of command. The owner or president of an organization would be great, but usually you can't get to them unless you network your way directly. A reasonable goal is to interview with the person who would be your boss and maybe some co-workers as well.

This approach will save you time, as taking an interview with a low-level pre-screener (say, a personnel assistant) makes you a low-priority candidate for the job. The pre-screener has one goal: to weed out most of the job applicants and pass on just a few who look exceptionally good. "Looking exceptionally good" is a subjective judgment; the pre-screener probably looks for people with nearly identical past experience to the job in question, reasoning that such experience is necessary for doing the job. This can make it hard for you to break into a job at a higher level or to change careers if you don't have official relevant experience.

Sometimes you can't avoid Human Resources, especially with bureaucratic government and educational jobs. But in business, it's best to aim high in the interview process in order to quickly get yourself in front of people who can hire you.

Getting interviews for jobs is a full-time job in itself. There are a number of tested ways to get interviews. Many of them involve using your network of professional contacts, but others rely much more on maintaining a constant awareness of how to take advantage of golden opportunities, whether you are expecting them or not. Sometimes your best interview is the one you didn't recognize!

The interview you didn't even know was an interview

The dynamism and informality of many workplaces, the need to make decisions quickly without spending lots of money and involving lots of people, and the rapid pace of growth and employee turnover in some firms—all these factors have remade the job interview, making it less stiff and proper.

Every new acquaintance gives you the chance to present yourself professionally with the thought that this person may provide a lead to a job. Of course, as you become more experienced in your career, you'll be helping others in exactly this way—this is what keeps a network alive. Be ready to share your ideas and contacts when the time is appropriate.

Here's a little story to illustrate how informal interviews may happen. Maria, a well-educated young woman who speaks several languages and has an interest in international business, once sat next to a businessman on a flight to Europe. They chatted and found some mutual interests. Maria listened carefully and asked the man a question: "What is your greatest problem?" She considered his answer and told him how she would solve that problem. By the time she got off the plane, she had a managerial job working for his company—a job she kept for a number of years and at which she was very successful. Her boss knew from the start that Maria was a natural problem-solver.

The interview where no job is available, so everyone is relaxed

This is, in many ways, the ideal situation. You are not even looking for a job; the employer is not looking for a new hire. Neither of you is on edge, and you can talk as equals. If the chemistry is right, you've planted a seed that might germinate and come to harvest at the right time.

Most casual jobs at restaurants, retail stores and the like are found this way—you go in and ask around until you find an immediate need or hit it off well with someone who will keep you in mind.

Here's what happened to Alice: Alice had a friend who worked for Goldman Sachs. Alice was a clothing designer, with no particular interest in finance. But when her friend's boss decided to start an investment program for the fashion industry, her friend began talking with Alice about what the program should look like. By the time the investment program was in place, Alice was the assistant director.

The interview you got by chance, by persistence, or by proxy

Often all the so-called rules of getting interviews are overturned by a job-seeker's determination or good reputation. In some cases, the candidate's resume was either wrong for the job or didn't measure up to the resumes submitted by other candidates. Other times, the candidate's reputation is so inspirational that jobs come to him or her effortlessly, by someone else's doing. The lessons here are 1) to persist until you get a definite "no" for an opening, and to accept the "no" graciously—you might be the person they call next time and 2) to be prepared for the pleasant experience of having someone else be your champion in the job search.

Consider Pat's story: Pat worked for the U.S. Census Bureau in upstate New York as an interviewer. She had to quit the job and wanted them to hire her friend Kelly. She recommended Kelly to her boss at the Census Bureau. He phoned Kelly from Boston and hired her on the phone. Of course, Kelly still had to take and pass a Civil Service exam, which she did. But she really had the job when her friend recommended her. Kelly had the unexpected pleasure of having a job handed to her.

Or look at Kim's experience: Recent college graduate Kim saw a job in the help wanted ads and applied to be a career counseling intern at a prestigious private university in the next town. She liked the collegiate atmosphere and thought she'd enjoy counseling. The problem was she could not get an interview. In fact, the man hiring had closed the position after not being able to hire the person he had wanted. He had seen Kim's resume but was not impressed by it. Kim didn't know any of this, so she kept calling his office till she reached the man at his desk. He shuffled through the pile of resumes and found hers. He asked Kim some questions about the resume, then started asking her who she knew in town. They found a common friend; he called the friend; a few minutes later he called Kim back and scheduled her for an interview the next day. Kim found out later that the friend spoke very well of her and that the man hiring had essentially decided to give her the job based on that recommendation.

Here's what happened to Josh: Josh was not looking for a new job in a serious way, but his boss was leaving their workplace and wanted to help Josh get a better job before he left. He found a promising job in a trade newspaper's "help wanted" section, called Jerry (who was doing the hiring) and talked about Josh. Josh's boss and Jerry were graduates of the same university and had several other common interests. By the time they got off the phone, Jerry was scheduling Josh for a round of interviews. He liked Josh's boss, and was willing to think Josh might be the same type of person in some ways. Josh got that job and was quite successful in it.

Job interview situations to avoid as much as possible

Sometimes you can't control every part of the interview screening process. The organization may have a rigid format developed to satisfy all legal requirements. Other times, the job in question is being used as a political football, and the interview schedule keeps getting postponed. But there are some ways you can avoid going after interviews that will not necessarily be productive.

#1: The interview where either you or the interviewer has not done their homework

Be sure you meet minimum qualifications for a job before your interview or figure out a way to negotiate what you don't have in exchange for your willingness to be trained or to start in a different position and move sideways, etc. Understand that in big organizations, you may be interviewing with people who know very little about the job you are pursuing. Be prepared to speak for yourself if the interviewer has no questions for you, and be sure that you have some carefully-prepared questions for your interviewer.

Being completely unqualified for a job can be downright embarrassing. Molly decided that she wanted to work in a dental office because she enjoyed having her teeth cleaned. She answered an ad for a dental hygienist and was called in for an interview. The first question concerned her training as a dental hygienist. Where did she go to school? "School? Why, I . . . thought you'd train me on the job." The dentist was kind, but Molly felt like a fool.

Jason had a three-day series of interviews for a college administrator position. He saw 18 people in various areas of the college. One of them was the comptroller. He had no clear idea why Jason was there to see him. It was very awkward until Jason chanced upon one of the comptroller's enthusiasms—the "ball" chair that he used at his computer. This led to a high-level lecture of computer technology that Jason listened to respectfully, saving the day for both of them. The comptroller was pleased to recommend Jason based on their interaction, and Jason got the job.

#2: *The interview they have to give you: a legal obligation*

In the US, Equal Opportunity laws mandate that certain positions be advertised at certain times in certain ways and that a reasonable number of qualified candidates be interviewed for every position.

This seems like a good idea, except that you may end up in an interview for which a very well-qualified person who already works at the organization has been chosen for a promotion. You may not know this, but what it means to you is that your interview is pro forma. Such interviews may feel false and trivial. Nothing is at stake, so no difficult questions are asked. It's like a bad blind date; courtesy forces you to go through the motions of a social interaction, but there's no urgency or true need involved, so the interview is flat.

#3: *The courtesy interview*

Sometime the interview is not destined to end with a possible job offer simply because there is no job open at the moment. However, you can make such an interview productive by asking your interviewer if she has any ideas where you might be a good fit in another organization. She may give you a referral that may lead to a new round of interviews. You could ask her for feedback on your interview performance. If you get along well, she may remember you at some future date when her company has a job opening.

Consider Kevin: Kevin's mother knew the president of a local bank socially. She persistently asked the president to meet with Kevin about a job until the president said "yes" just to get some peace. The interview was perfectly polite but with no depth, as the president had no real interest in Kevin's qualifications. Kevin wisely used the time as an information interview in which he gained knowledge about working in a bank. Because Kevin had made a good impression on the president, he got a referral to another bank that was hiring, and he got the job.

"And do you have any questions for us?"

Often job-seekers become so focused on being able to anticipate and respond to the employer's questions that they forget that interviews are conversations. Yet it's just as important to ask good questions as to give intelligent answers. You will stand out from other candidates if your questions reveal a working knowledge of the industry and specific knowledge about the organization itself.

This is another place where your ability to do thorough research will pay off. It's simple enough to find out where the industry in question is headed, be it finance, manufacturing, entertainment, the law, education, religious organizations, hospitality, medical services, or any other big player in the economy. Trade and international newspapers, specialized online media, public records on annual industry performance and predictions, and non-profit reports can give you an accurate idea of what is happening around the organization that you are researching.

Data on the organization itself comes from many of the same kinds of sources. From all this information, you can craft intelligent questions that reveal your in-depth knowledge of the problems and possibilities that confront the employer and the industry. Typical questions might center on these topics:

- Who is your main competition?

- What long-term strategies do you have for this department?

- How are outside factors like regulation, taxation, and the labor supply affecting your organization?

- Does this department favor an individual or team approach to new projects?

- What kind of professional development opportunities are available to employees?

- What is a typical career path in your organization?

- What are the organization's core values?

- What is the process for professional evaluations?

- What support facilities are available for this department (laboratories, equipment, computers)?

Note that it's always wise to have an idea of the answers to these questions so that you avoid embarrassing the employer or yourself by asking a question that seems too pointed or reveals a sore spot. If you appear to know too much, you can arouse the employer's suspicions about how you gained that knowledge.

Avoid asking questions that will seem trivial or naïve. Your questions should spring naturally from what you have learned from your research. If you have no questions, it may be that you have not exercised your imagination about this job. What do you really want to know? How could the answers affect your continued interest in the job either positively or negatively?

If you have developed good rapport in the interview, consider asking this question: "What is your greatest problem, and how can I help you solve it?" You don't want to put the employer on the spot or seem to be boasting about your abilities, so use this question only if you have the confidence that it will be seen as sincere. If asked at the right time in the right way, it could be the question that gets you the job.

The changing face of job interviewing

Some sources say that 1/3 of all Americans move each year. A significant number of job changes are happening all the time: people get fired, relocated, or laid off; they quit; get married, retire, move abroad, or change career fields. With such constant change, job interviews emphasize efficiency over formality. People have job interviews by Skype, telephone, email, FedEx, and in airport hotels where interviewer and interviewee each travel halfway.

Chris's experience is not unusual. Twice, Chris did consulting work for people she never met. In one instance, she had been recommended by a friend for the job. There was no interview; Chris simply answered an email that asked her for her availability. She did everything by computer and never spoke directly with anyone involved, either in person or by telephone. Her pay went straight into her bank account, so she never saw a check from her employer. For another job, Chris received checks signed by the US Secretary of State, but the Secretary certainly didn't hire Chris or even know who she was. The program was handled by a government contractor who was hired by the Department of State on a per-project basis. Chris was never interviewed by anyone or met any of the people involved in the program except the participants, who flew from their native countries to Washington, then on to her city, where she delivered a two-week professional development program for them. Chris submitted a bid for each program in the form of a written proposal and only worked when her proposal was accepted. Everything except for the programs themselves was done by email and an occasional phone call.

Interviews are a special type of conversation

The interview, however relaxed it may seem, has just one purpose from the perspective of the employer: to quickly assess the job-related strengths and weaknesses of the candidate and to imagine the candidate working in the organization.

What seem like perfectly normal questions are often traps for the unwary; the more cordial and friendlier the interviewer, the more likely an inexperienced job-seeker is to walk straight into the trap. In addition, it's quite likely that the interviewer is not a full-time interviewer with lots of experience in putting people at ease and all the time in the world to listen to rambling answers. He or she may be your potential boss or a human resources person with many other responsibilities. Your ability to stick to the point in the interview will be welcome.

Here are some common interview questions:

- Tell me about yourself.

- In what period of your life did you feel the most successful? The least successful?

- What do your accomplishments communicate about your values and beliefs?

- How have you influenced others?

- What past jobs have you had, and how did you like them?

- What are your career goals?

- What are your greatest strengths? Weaknesses?

- What would your best friend say about you? Your worst enemy?

- Have your accomplishments been deliberate or accidental?

- Describe a team situation that worked well in your life. Now describe one that didn't work well.

- What personal characteristics do you have that are of the greatest value to your friends?

- What good qualities did you inherit or learn from your family?

- What have you been praised for in your life? What have you been criticized for?

- Who are your heroes? Why?

- Describe something you created or designed that gave you a strong sense of satisfaction. Why did you feel satisfied about it?

These questions look easy, but let's take a closer look at them.

#1: *"Tell me about yourself."*

This is a common opener and your chance to establish your framework for the interview. The interviewer most likely already has some basic facts from your resume, so this is not really an information-sharing question. Rather, it's the first time the interviewer can talk with you in person, in action.

The bits of information you share about yourself begin with what's on the resume. This is safe, as the interviewer probably has this information already and has decided to interview you. Starting with some nice, non-emotional facts makes you more confident. If you feel unsure, you can always ask for feedback— "is there anything in particular you'd like me to explain?"—if you sense the interviewer has a specific agenda.

If your first interview is on the telephone or via computer, then you have to be even more careful of what you say and how you say it. Humor rarely travels well, so don't try for whimsy or cuteness. Be straightforward and concise in your responses.

The cardinal rule of interviews is "never say anything negative." The smallest criticism or complaint at this point becomes your identity. Never mind that the criticism is fully justified; the interviewer will assume, if you criticize anyone not in the room at the moment, that you'll do the same to him or her when you leave the room. This is a bad way to start a relationship.

There's an unspoken agreement between employer and employee that each will contribute a certain amount of loyalty to each other. (This agreement is weakening as the world economy continues to cause upheavals in the workplace, but it's still best to proceed as if it were true.) This loyalty includes, to a certain degree, the notion that you keep a united front to the world that your organization is doing just fine, thank you. Interviewers want to know how much loyalty they can expect from you. Of course, this mutual loyalty may be frayed or broken due to changed circumstances when you actually work there, but at least in the interview, you need to show a willingness to defend the people in your life from criticism.

If you have any past experiences that were not entirely positive, take time before the interview to devise a way to speak gently of that experience. For instance, if you were fired from a job for any reason (even if you weren't at fault), and the interviewer asks about it, focus on what you learned in that job and move on.

#2: *"What are your career goals?"*

This is the most important question of all for the interviewer who's seriously interested in you. Although an organization may promise upward mobility, at the moment the interviewer is only trying to fill the job in question. It's reassuring to the interviewer when your career goals nicely mesh with the job. Your career goals must have some connection with the job you want, or you are wasting your time, and the time of the interviewer. Tailor your goals accordingly.

Think about what Matt experienced when he wanted to hire a new secretary. He had gone to the trouble to write a thorough job description which was available to every candidate. This job required a secretary who could use a computer to organize his appointments and type his correspondence. Yet Matt interviewed people whose career goal was to be a cook or an art teacher. He was amazed that these people took the time to interview for a job that they had no interest in—and to tell him so!

Another common problem for career-changers is to switch gears from their past to the new job they seek. Jill, an elementary-school teacher for two decades, was training to be a paralegal in a two-year college program. She wanted to get a part-time job or internship in a law firm for experience and to make contacts. Her resume was five pages long and covered all her accolades and accomplishments as a teacher. Jill needed to make a one-page qualifications brief that focused on the communication, organizational, and writing skills that a law firm would welcome.

Instead, she gave the impression that she was looking for another teaching job

#3: *"What are your greatest strengths? Weaknesses?"*

This is a classic interview question. For the "greatest strength," you should have a nice, brief story prepared to illustrate your communication or organizational skills, or whatever is appropriate for the job. For your weaknesses, choose one that's not fatal to the performance of the job—for example, you can confess to weak chemistry skills if the job doesn't call for them. Avoid statements such as "I just work too hard! I'm always the last person to leave the office!"; you may sound insincere.

The Bottom Line

Interviews are conversations about the current needs of an organization and your professional skills and accomplishments. The purpose of the conversation is for both sides to get to know each other well enough to see if there might be a match. What are their most pressing problems at the moment? How can you solve their problems as quickly and economically as possible?

Interviewing can seem like this: you are looking for a slot into which you will fit with little or no adjustment., and the employer is looking for the same thing—an easy fix. It's all about perceptions on both sides: you want to present yourself as the person who can solve their problems, and they want to show you just enough of their true needs to entice you into working for them. Interviewing can seem almost mechanical, as the emphasis is so strongly on the professional *you* and so little on the personal *you*. Try to keep a proper perspective on this crucial moment in the job-search process.

Don't forget, in all your preparation and pursuit of the perfect job at the perfect place, that people are at the heart of everyone's career. People have educated you, communicated with you, helped you, challenged you, corrected you, encouraged you, and guided you since the moment of your creation. Ultimately, every job, even the most technical, is about people, as people will either benefit or suffer from the results.

Remember, too, that people hire people, not skill sets. Although the job search seems to be all about qualifications and requirements, as if getting a job is an equation to be balanced, it's really about finding a work setting in which you and the people already employed can work in harmony and accord to make something worthwhile, be it a product, a service, or an idea.

Regardless of whether you are working face-to-face, on a computer via a satellite relay, across a landscape of cell phone towers, or through old-fashioned written documents, you are working with people. Respecting diversity, finding commonality, seeing things from many perspectives, refusing to feel threatened by seeming-intractable differences, turning problems into opportunities—these are the vital interpersonal skills that never go out of fashion.

.   .   .   .

Steps to Reinventing Your Future

1. What are three significant ways you can prepare for an interview?

2. How do potential employers screen you as a job candidate to find out what's not on the resume: your attitude, interpersonal skills, degree of tact, loyalty, and day-to-day willingness to do what needs to be done at work?

3. How do you as a job candidate find out about the advantages and disadvantages of working in the industry, organization, and job you are interviewing for? What kinds of questions must you prepare for the interview so that you will have something worthwhile to say when it's your turn to talk?

Chapter Five: Working abroad: putting your communication and decision-making skills to the test

In our increasingly interdependent global economy of the 21st century, keeping your passport handy is a feature of daily life for those who are fully aware of their own potential and have decided to pursue career opportunities abroad. As they move from one country to the next, they count on having a current, valid passport to verify their identity and demonstrate their right to be wherever a new assignment may take them.

Getting a national passport is a routine bureaucratic procedure, but choosing and pursuing your golden opportunities in the global economy requires more than just filling in forms and paying a fee. What is required for being successful in an international job search? You will need to produce your career passport, the one that you must have to compete and thrive in the world of work beyond your national borders. Building your career passport will require intensive research, serious skill evaluation and development, and extensive preparation. Once you have made up your mind to explore working and living outside your native country, you will find a wide range of prospects in the job market, but you will also find that the level of competence needed to compete against the other highly-qualified applicants can only be attained through hard work and focused determination. In this chapter, we intend to encourage you but also to challenge you to bring your very best game when you look for a job abroad.

Chapters Two, Three, and Four of *Reinventing Your Future* outline the basic tasks of the job search: self-knowledge, career research, written communications, and interview preparation. When you have created your career portfolio by working through and mastering all the exercises and advice in these chapters, you have a basis for looking for a job in your home country.

But if you decide to look for a job in another country, you will find that you need considerably more preparation than just the basics. Most of this preparation is mental: creative thinking and developing outstanding decision-making skills are crucial skills to master. In addition, preparation is needed in terms of attitude: flexibility to deal with emerging situations, a non-judgmental mindset to appreciate the differences in a new country, and independence of spirit to solve the problems of operating in a culture that's not your own.

Naturally, you will need a complete package of marketable skills tailored to the specific needs of the country in which you have chosen to live and work. You will be competing with local people and with other expatriates (expats) for interviews and offers in a relatively small pool of jobs. The laws of most countries make it harder for an employer to hire a foreign worker; your skills have to be exactly what's needed for the jobs you are pursuing so that the employer can justify hiring you rather than a native. You will need to do extensive research to know what to offer, to whom, and how, if you expect to get hired abroad.

Note: if you are being transferred by the organization where you work, you have some distinct advantages and disadvantages. While you may not need to find a job and may receive corporate support such as financial help with the costs of moving your possessions, renting accommodations, and family allowances, you will not have as much flexibility as the person who is doing it all on his or her own.

Our professional qualifications concerning working and living abroad

The International Leadership Institute has maintained operations both in the US and Europe since its establishment it in 1985. In these years, we've traveled extensively in Central Europe (the Czech and Slovak Republics, Germany, Switzerland, Hungary, and Austria) and the US. Our main offices have been located at various times in New Jersey, New York, Tennessee, Georgia, Florida, and Prague. We understand what it means to work and live abroad, both from our own experience and from working with thousands of people in their career and leadership development.

Institute President Jarda Tusek's pre-1985 career spanned seven countries on two continents. From his native land of Czechoslovakia, where he grew up in Prague, Jarda began his international career in 1966. He first tapped into his networks to find a job in West Germany; there he earned money to fund his move to Norway, where he attended the University of Oslo to research his doctoral dissertation for the Charles University School of Law in Prague, where he was a student. Czechoslovakia was, at that time, a closed Soviet bloc country where incomes were very low; his West German earnings helped him get established in Norway.

Jarda already spoke German and had German friends, along with knowledge of German history, art, and literature, so he fit into his German job with few problems. In the meantime, he studied Norway: the literature, language, law, history, culture, music, and geography. He learned a bit of Norwegian and worked there briefly one summer to get a perspective on the country and its people. When he moved from Germany to Norway, he found a job washing dishes, then went on to working at the University of Oslo as a nattvakt (night watch in the student dormitories) and volleyball coach; he also coached and traveled around Europe with the Norwegian National Volleyball team. He was significantly helped by his knowledge of German, French, and English while living in Norway. Although he did not begin in an executive position, he steadily improved his career as he made friends, built new networks, and added to his understanding of Norway and the people who lived there.

From his Norwegian experience, Jarda gained confidence, new skills, new networks of contacts, and a bigger vision of the world. He used his educational achievements, language skills, and ability to adapt quickly to changing circumstances to find creative,

productive professional work in Norway, Switzerland, England,

Germany, Canada, the Czech Republic, and the United States. In

every country where he lived and worked, Jarda studied the arts,

literature, history, language, geography, and economy in order to

situate himself within the culture of that particular place and time.

His jobs included research at the International Peace Research

Institute in Oslo, consulting at the World Council of Churches in

Geneva, pursuing a postgraduate fellowship in international

economics at the Institute of International Studies of the University

of Geneva, refugee assistance for Czechs and Slovaks in England,

directing young adult career programs in Canada, California, and

North Carolina for the American Management Association, and

directing career services offices in New York and Georgia.

Jarda used his own international career when he envisioned

the International Leadership Institute as an organization devoted to

helping professionals develop their leadership skills in international

settings. From its establishment in 1985, the Institute has worked

with thousands of individuals from a wide range of countries and industries to make it possible for them to attain professional success in their chosen industries.

American Sara Tusek, Managing Director of the Institute, began her international career in 1990 when she first traveled to Czechoslovakia. The country was just beginning to turn away from its communist past and take its place internationally. From 1990-2010, Sara and Jarda ran the Institute from the US with lengthy business trips to Europe in order to find program partners and participants for Institute programs, including the *Business Leadership Forum: USA*, *American English Language Institute*, *Travel-and-Learn* programs, ILI trade missions, and *Reinventing Your Future* career development workshops. Sara and Jarda lived in Prague from 2010-2013; in those years, Sara focused on international education and publishing. Prior to that, Sara directed career services at a private Tennessee university, taught English and Writing on the college and secondary school levels, and worked with thousands of foreign students in their pursuit of excellence in American English, helping them establish themselves in international careers. She is the Executive Editor of International Leadership Institute Publications, a publisher of books, articles, educational materials, and reports aimed at inspiring and assisting people in the areas of international leadership and career development, improvement of English language skills, and the political and economic changes of the 21st century.

We've also incorporated the insights and perspectives of more than 15,000 career-minded individuals we've counseled and instructed in the past five decades. Many of these ambitious people went on to careers that spanned countries and continents, building on the knowledge, skills, and attitudes we helped them discover, develop, and refine. Through the International Leadership Institute and our involvement as program partners, students, and employees with more than 30 universities in the US and abroad, we have extensive and varied experience with people whose career goals involve working internationally.

Key insights into successfully building an international career

We've studied the career trajectories of successful entrepreneurs, Olympic athletes, diplomats, corporate executives, and professionals such as lawyers, physicians, university professors, journalists, and clergy. In so doing, we've identified three key areas of competence that are essential for finding a job abroad and performing in that job with distinction:

#1: *Flexibility in working conditions and a non-judgmental attitude*

The first prerequisite is openness to what's not familiar. Most of us have a plethora of well-defined daily habits, both in action and in thinking. Working in a country where you did not grow up will challenge each of your habits. The mealtimes, language, food, length of the work day, hours for sleeping, customs for socializing with co-workers, healthcare and health insurance, holidays, transportation, costs of daily items, tax rates (both local and from your native country), ways of making friends, banking, postal system—all of it is different. While you may think that you can easily adjust and believe that the adjusting is part of the grand adventure of working abroad, the sheer magnitude of the adjustments can be overwhelming. Everywhere you turn, you are reminded that you are out-of-step with the people around you.

What's even more challenging is the matter of your own attitude. It becomes easy to get irritated with "the locals" and blame all miscommunications on their ignorance, stubbornness, or sheer willfulness—they persist in being themselves in the face of your exhaustion at trying to make sense of their behavior!

We've experienced these job-related complaints from ourselves or our expat friends: the bathrooms are filthy; the boss gives no positive feedback, only criticism; there are unstated "extra" duties like coming in early to unlock the offices and clean the common areas; it's almost impossible to negotiate with suppliers and deal with irate customers when your language skills are not well-developed; or the boss expects you to help her children with their schoolwork in English as part of your entirely-different job. You may find yourself dealing with the Foreign Police (whose rules are not as clear as you might like) about your visa/change of address/landlord who says he never heard of you. You are suddenly chastised for rudeness over some incident that you don't even remember, so you can't explain your side.

These differences in everyday life are, of course, part of the reason you want to work abroad. And from a distance, all these problems seem trifling. But they accumulate and can lead to frustration, discouragement, and a bad attitude toward the very people (your employer, your co-workers, and friends) whose help you most need.

It's essential to do your homework before you leave home. Take yourself seriously—learn some basic vocabulary in the language where you want to live. Study the culture—learn about the history, artistic achievements, literature, geography, religion, economy, political system, and place in the world of your new country. Travel once you get there—learn about the diversity of its people, food, customs, and pressing issues. Find out what's expected of you in your new country. In Switzerland, for example, there are four important languages spoken in various parts of the country, and professionals should know at least the basics of each one. Your career will thrive or struggle to survive based on your ability to fit in to your new home and communicate with your co-workers and your boss.

#2: *The ability to communicate effectively in a language and/or culture that is not native to you.*

The second necessary skill set is communications. In spite of all your efforts to learn the language of your country of choice, you may at least at first speak the language like a toddler. The natural tendency is to find expats from "back home" who speak your language, but try to move beyond that. Speaking the native language even imperfectly helps you feel better integrated and shows the people around you that you want to know them. Becoming fluent in their language is key to success in business and professional settings.

Maybe the language spoken in your new country is your own, but the subtle differences will trip you up. British English and American English, for example, are mutually understandable, but the fine points are so different that you may unintentionally be comical or offensive. Don't assume that you are communicating well just because you understand words; real meaning is found in intention and context.

Often, especially in business, people communicate in a third language that is neither's native tongue. Here great tact and discretion are called for, as nuance is distorted. Simple customs may differ: does one speaker finish a sentence before the other replies, or is there excited, enthusiastic interruption? How formally or informally can you communicate with others? The ability to gauge social distinctions and maintain courtesy is a function of language combined with observation and discreet questioning. Making mistakes in these situations can be very troublesome.

#3: An above-average skill set in the field you are working in

The third absolute prerequisite is knowing your stuff—having a solid set of skills in the career field of choice. You need to check on the certifications, degrees, diplomas, and experience that are required and customary in the country where you plan to work. Some degrees and certifications don't transfer; physicians, nurses, lawyers, university professors, engineers, clergy, scientists, accountants, and many other professionals may have to take exams and courses in the language of the country or pay professional registration fees (both initially and annually). Generally, business is less interested in credentials but more interested in language fluency.

Practicalities

You could get by without knowing much about the history, artistic and scientific achievements, educational system, literature and music, political and economic systems, and relationship to neighboring countries of your chosen country, but why would you not be curious about the riches to be found? Taking time to situate your country of choice pays benefits when you live there. You can better interpret the attitudes you will encounter and avoid insulting your new friends with your ignorance (which may seem like arrogance) about the achievements and distinguishing marks of their native land.

We already mentioned healthcare and health insurance but want to emphasize the need to be responsible about taking care of yourself. If you need insulin, for example, how will you get your supplies? Do you need to buy health insurance, or does your job/university provide it? Which doctors will see you if you buy foreigner's health insurance? Are the medications you take considered OTC (over the counter) or prescription only?

Legalities like visas, passport renewal, work permits, taxes at home and abroad, absentee voting in your native country, the possibilities of obtaining citizenship in your chosen country—all of these are serious matters. What's more, they may be confusing, as laws change often and without warning. Consider the uncertainty in 2019 surrounding British citizens working abroad during the Brexit negotiations. Finding a competent lawyer can help you obey the laws. Should you decide to marry, you will have a host of questions; some may be answered by the embassy or consulate of your own country. Research this information before you leave your home country.

Using your decision-making skills

We assume at this point that you have your up-to-date career portfolio. You have completed Chapters Two, Three, and Four in *Reinventing Your Future*, reading the advice and doing all the exercises. Without a firm understanding of the current job market in your country of choice, your own abilities, accomplishments and values, how to communicate in writing and in interviews, and the importance of networks, you will find working abroad to be a hard nut to crack. Everything that's true of competing in your home country is doubly true when you are competing in a country where you have distinct disadvantages.

Back home, you had friends, family members, former teachers and pastors, neighbors, and a host of people who knew you and had a stake in your success. You had a level of comfort in daily routines and an innate sense of what was happening in social situations. Your background knowledge about your country's history helped you correctly interpret new developments, and your familiarity with various regional accents gave you flexibility in your native language. All that is gone now. Or is it?

Perhaps the most challenging and demanding task for you is, not surprisingly, to quickly build your interpersonal and communication skills. All the chores of daily life are no longer automatic; finding a place to live, buying food, hooking up your utilities and phone service, learning how to get from here to there are all different from back home. But the good news is that all these chores are helping you build your new network of friends, neighbors, and potential job leads.

And at the same time, you are developing valuable skills of cross-cultural communication that make it possible for you to stand outside your own small world of personal experience and see things very differently. As weeks and months go by, your new routines will become more natural, and you will start to relax into your new identity as an expat. You will move from being a "babe in the woods" who gets upset at every challenge into being a less impulsive, more thoughtful, and significantly wiser member of society. In your job, you will make friends and take on more responsibilities as you better grasp what's important and what is not.

You'll find that your decision-making skills have broadened and deepened as you add different ways of evaluating situations. Your colleagues and co-workers are new role models who can change you in profound and lasting ways. What may have begun on a whim—to work abroad—will surely have consequences in your career far beyond what you can imagine today.

. . . .

Steps to Reinventing Your Future

1. Why would an organization hire a non-native for a particular job?

2. Are there any potential problems or advantages for you working legally in the country you are considering?

3. How will you fund your job search? Is it always feasible to have a job all lined up when you move aboard?

4. What are three considerations of daily life that you find most crucial to your job performance and general satisfaction in working abroad?

5. List several positive reasons for working abroad. Then list some disadvantages, including people and career opportunities you will miss in your home country.

6. How will your jobs in another country fit into your long-term career goals?

Chapter Six: Your new job—evaluating offers and settling in

At some point, the interviews you have taken will begin to help you make sense of your job search. If you get interviews but no offers, you may need to revise your career or job goals. Perhaps you aren't as suited for a job as you had originally imagined, or you found, at closer range, this was not the job for you. Maybe the economy is not open for new hires in the jobs you seek. You may be thinking about going to graduate school, making a geographical move, or changing your career goal altogether.

This is an important juncture. The interviews have given you feedback on your own "job fit" in particular jobs and a picture of the market and the economy, which are in a state of constant change, as they affect the job you seek. You may have received one or more offers and now have more information on which to base an intelligent assessment of the offer.

Job offer analysis and comparison

One way to make a rational comparison of potential jobs is to list the top ten factors that you want to consider in your new job. Here are some considerations:

- Job skills needed, both at entry-level and above;

- Position of organization within its profession: industry leader, cutting edge, or well-established;

- Methods of employee assessment, retention, and promotion;

- Job-related education and training opportunities, especially those that are employer-funded;

- Geographical location and possibilities for relocation;

- Co-workers: your perceived ability to get along with those you would work with daily;

- Company or organization values and mission: how well do they match your own values and career goals?

- Financial considerations: salary and benefits, including 401K accounts, pensions, and other retirement benefits: don't ask about these at the first interview, but try to get the information some other way;

- Vacation time/sick time/health insurance and other benefits;

- Expenses to begin the job: relocation, selling or buying a house, buying a car, etc.;

- Opinion of and impact on your family and/or friends;

- Intangibles such as job fit and chemistry that can't be quantified but have a significant influence on job satisfaction and performance.

Assign each factor a number indicating its relative importance (#1 being more important, etc.). Take each job offer and assess it according to your top ten. Obviously, the job with the highest score wins! But if you are not satisfied with your winning job, keep at it until you are reasonably sure that you are choosing a job you like and can do best.

You also need to consider the less objective parts of the job, such as your feelings about the job's environment and the closeness of the match between the job and your goals. These aspects of the job become crucial, making life easier or harder when you have to do chores and tasks that are distasteful to you. A thorough analysis of the job offer or offers using such a list can save you expense and dissatisfaction. Give serious thought to how accepting this job offer would change your life.

How to get off to a great start in your new job!

There's a certain excitement that comes with beginning a new job. Since the page is blank, so to speak, there's feeling that you can write whatever you want on it, and this will become your job. Being new brings a few privileges—people may be willing to take time to help you and show you the informal systems of the organization. You won't be part of any faction and will be spared office politics. You can do your job in peace and quiet without the distractions of your previous job and get off to a clean start.

This may all be true, but then again, maybe not; being new has its risks. The downsizing of Human Resources departments in recent years has often eliminated the welcoming and integration of new employees in a formal orientation. As a result, it's quite possible that no one person is in charge of helping you figure out where you are and what you should be doing. Office politics won't stop just because you have arrived. You may be expected to fit in on your own; your ability to adjust is part of your unofficial orientation. Do you have what it takes to work there?

Take your cues from your boss, or the person who hired you-- but that's not always so easy!

Consider Kyle's experience with his new job. It took months for him to find out how to get his employee code for the electronic alarm system and the copy machine. No one told him about the free coffee in Room 222 every morning or the monthly staff Sunday brunch at a local restaurant. It's not that anyone deliberately excluded Kyle, but no one thought to tell him. They didn't think of it as their responsibility to orient him; they just assumed he knew what they knew.

Here's what happened to Taylor. His new boss, Alicia, was not in her office on his first day on the job. She was in Utah for three weeks with a new client, according to her secretary. Unsure of what to do, Taylor found Mike, who'd been on the interviewed team.

Fortunately for Taylor, even though it wasn't Mike's responsibility, Mike took him to Human Resources to sign up for payroll and benefits, which had barely been mentioned in the interview process. Mike then showed Taylor to an empty desk and gave him a small research project to get him started. Later that day, Alicia called Mike for a quote for her client, and he reminded her that Taylor was now on the job. She had forgotten about Taylor in the rush to get to Utah. She thanked Mike and called Taylor.

In a busy company it's quite possible that no one will be available to orient or train a new employee. Human Resources may offer some kinds of training on technical jobs (usually online), but new hires for administrative and managerial jobs are often handled within their departments, which may or may not have the time to provide a good orientation.

Getting used to the organizational climate

Especially for someone at her first job after college, adjusting to a new way of accomplishing work takes flexibility and initiative. At college and in many bureaucratic jobs, the parameters are very clear. The work day begins and ends at a scheduled time; the tasks are spelled out; the results are reviewed, and feedback is given on a regular basis.

Ellen's experience illustrates the need to fit into a new job. Ellen had been an Anthropology major in college; since the Anthropology department was small, she knew her professors well. She was a star student and hired as a research assistant. She was very good at following directions and doing what she was told.

Ellen's new job was in a marketing firm. Her job title was Marketing Assistant, and she was assigned to a team with seven other employees. She came to work at 8:30 in the morning the first day, as directed, and found that everyone else had been there since 7. The team was rushing to finish a complicated proposal for a key client, and no one had time to talk with Ellen. She watched for a few minutes and then offered to help Tim, who was transferring some data to another computer. He gave her a few words of explanation, and Ellen dove into the project. No one stopped for lunch—they had sandwiches brought in—and no one left at 5. Ellen followed their lead and stayed till 6:30, when the team decided to go out for dinner and talk over what they needed to do tomorrow. Ellen was now an official team member; the team climate was work hard, play hard, and she fit in.

Here are a few key suggestions for initial success as you begin a new job.

#1: Solicit feedback

In the first few weeks, Anna felt uncomfortable to end each day with very little to show. In her previous job as an editorial assistant, she had been close to her boss, who trusted her judgment and let her work independently as long as the results were good. She was not held accountable for what she did every day. But her new job in textbook sales was quite different. Her boss, Tom, required a daily report on all of her activities and expected concrete gains.

Anna was getting nervous, as her reports didn't look stellar. But rather than wait to be scolded, Anna met with Tom and asked for feedback. She was relieved to hear that Tom understood that she needed some time to learn the job before she made sales. With her newly-gained confidence, Anna persevered and became a valuable employee.

#2: Take initiative: ask for what you need to do your job

Anna soon found that her office-supplied cell phone, passed on from her predecessor, was not what she needed for the job. She requested and was given a new smartphone with a better data plan and longer battery life.

#3: Learn not to take things personally

Anna learned a valuable lesson from observing how her boss, Tom, reacted when he was passed over for a promotion. He was angry at first, remembering all he contributed to the firm. Then he decided to trust that Management had access to more information than he did, and their promotion policy might not be the same as his. He put aside his feelings and accepted that this was not a personal rebuke aimed at him. Anna saw that keeping your temper is sometimes the best response to an unclear situation.

#4: *Think teams, not mentors*

Anna had read an old job search book that advised her to look for a mentor. But she found that, in a busy environment, no one has extra time to lavish on one individual. The success of the team depends on everyone's sustained, productive efforts; there's no way to gently bring someone up to speed, as a mentor would do. Anna simply did her best to fit in and make her own contributions to the team. She never did find a mentor, but she did take time to help the new hires who came after her. Eventually she found her niche as a seasoned veteran who could gently steer new employees as to the ways of working in her office.

#5: *Don't just do what you're told*

As Anna felt more confident in her job, she began to bring ideas for new sales strategies to her boss, Tom. He used a few and was pleased with the results. Anna's value to the organization grew, and Tom gave her room to expand her job duties. She began looking for ways to streamline the team's work. As she focused on becoming a responsible team member, she found gaps that she could fill. Soon Anna found that she was becoming happier at work as she contributed energy, creative ideas, and a positive attitude.

A variety of jobs: the good and the bad

Although it might seem only logical to have a reliable method to match people with their dream jobs, the world does not work that way. Policies that apply rational job matching strategies have rarely worked, perhaps because forcing people to work in specific jobs violates a basic principle of individual freedom: the right to choose and reinvent your own future.

The old-fashioned way of finding a job is still what we recommend. Using the resources you've developed and gathered in your career portfolio, you start with a clear idea of your skills and career goals. You spend time in focused research on an organization or industry that interests you. From there, you identify job titles or positions that seem to be a good match for your skills, talents, values, and abilities. Armed with this knowledge, you tap into your networks and published job ads to start generating interviews. From the interviews, you get offers and take the one that you like best.

Special jobs

But there are times that you simply need a job, any job. Maybe you are new in town, between career jobs, waiting to go to graduate school, or just about ready to retire. In any event, all the effort to find the right job described so far just doesn't seem possible or worthwhile at the moment. You may need a special job.

#1: Emergency job:

You just got fired, quit your job, or moved far away. You're running out of money and need to find a cash flow. Take the first job that comes your way. An online jobs site is an efficient way to fill a job that doesn't require specific, high-level skills or extensive experience. Beware, though, of job opportunities that promise you'll make quick money or don't ask for any qualifications—if it sounds too good to be true, it probably is!

Karen had a good experience with her emergency job. She had been working on a grant-funded project that suddenly lost its funding. Needing an income immediately, she responded to a free community want ad listing posted on the Internet looking for a coordinator of volunteers in a non-profit organization. Karen submitted her resume electronically and was called for a personal interview. She was hired and worked there productively for a number of years, demonstrating that sometimes emergency jobs can work out well for all concerned.

#2: Dead-end job:

This job can be dead-end by nature (you can't advance till you get more education, as in being a dental assistant vs. being a dentist) or dead-end because of the workplace practices. Maybe the company only promotes certain types of people, such as family members. It's illegal to discriminate in hiring and promotion, but it's much harder to prove discrimination in promotion than in hiring. These jobs are truly only for emergencies as they don't hold much potential for career satisfaction.

#3: Boring job:

Most entry-level jobs, even professional jobs in a bank or law firm, can be boring. It stands to reason that the better-paid, more senior employees get to do the more interesting work. The boring stuff gets pushed down to the bottom—the new hire.

For example, Liza worked at a large architecture firm. Since she was a new hire, her job was to make models of buildings for the architects to take to their client sales pitches. She didn't much enjoy this job, but knew she had to pay her dues before rising in the firm. She worked hard, spoke with her supervisor about her work, and eventually was promoted to a job assisting a senior architect.

#4: The impossible job:

This special job is often found where office politics have grown out of control. No matter who takes this job, confusion and even failure will follow because the job is simply not a reasonable job.

An example: Jason had, over ten years, scooped up every available responsibility and created many new ones in an effort to gain power in his management job, thus becoming (he hoped) indispensable. When he was fired due to budget cuts, his job was split up. The best parts of his job were divided into two new mid-level jobs in different divisions. The left-over parts that nobody wanted were combined into an impossible job; there was no internal logic in the tasks and no apparent need for anyone to do the job.

Another example: Ashley was hired to run a program in a large non-profit agency. But the person who hired her died about three months later, and in the scramble to fill his job, Ashley ended up with a new boss who had long hated her program and wanted to close it. Ashley lasted a "courtesy" year, and then was fired in a trumped-up charge. It was an impossible job, as everything Ashley did was downplayed and ignored by her boss, who didn't really want her to succeed.

#6: The job nobody seems to have a handle on:

This is similar to the "Impossible" job, except that usually it isn't a result of a past problem. It's just that no one has taken the time to fully think through what the job involves. Many assistant jobs are like this in that the person being assisted has to let go of certain aspects of his or her job in order for the assistant to function. Sometimes it's hard to let go; sometimes the opposite is true—the assistant is supposed to assume tasks without ever being told to do so.

How to cope with a special job

Naturally, all jobs have some aspects of these special jobs. The best response to special problems is for you to take initiative. If it seems like a good idea, try having a brief clarification talk with your immediate boss about an area in which you need some guidance. Avoid going over your boss's head; this is out of line in many organizations. At the same time, you may decide to quietly activate your personal network, getting your name out there in a subtle way, knowing that special jobs often collapse without warning or can cause you constant frustration. You may want to keep your job search private, as some organizations will see a job search as an act of disloyalty.

The job you create for yourself through entrepreneurship

By far the best and most rewarding jobs are those that are tailored to your specific skills, ambitions, and experience. Starting your own business or non-profit organization will use all your skills and then some. Entrepreneurial ventures provide jobs not just for the founder but for many others. Although entrepreneurship has its special challenges, including lack of financial stability and the tendency to work around the clock just to get everything done, it's very satisfying to create an organization that does exactly what you envision.

Here's an illustration: after completing a *Business Leadership Forum: USA* executive education program (delivered by the International Leadership Institute to European business leaders), one young graduate started a business on a shoestring, with just eight employees. His firm grew into a highly-successful business based in the Czech Republic which now employing hundreds of people around the world. In Carter Henderson's *Free Enterprise Moves East: Doing Business from Prague to Vladivostok*, you can read an account of this business leader's experiences. (More info in **Resources**)

Two years into the job: a turning point. More education? A career switch? A geographical dilemma?

No matter how much or how little you like your new job, it's a good idea to stay there for a two-year minimum commitment. This gives you time to learn enough about the organization and your job duties to be able to decide whether or not you're in a good career fit. It takes about a year to get over being the new person and gain some confidence in your ability to make a valuable contribution to the work setting. The second year, as you won't be so focused on yourself, you can evaluate the political and economic aspects, both internal and external, of the organization and get a feeling for where your employer is heading. At that point, you can reasonably assess your future in your job and organization.

There are numerous solutions to job dissatisfaction. You may be able to shift your job duties within your organization or transfer geographically if your organization has different locations. Look around for any unfilled need—that could be your new job in disguise, just waiting for you to exercise your imagination. If you are getting restless in your job, be sure to think before you act. Be comfortable with the pace and magnitude of change in your career, whether you choose the change or not. Rely on your critical thinking and problem-solving skills in order to plan.

Mid-life career crisis: the gap between your original dreams and your present situation

The mid-life crisis is a cliché, but it is also a fact of life for nearly everyone who works. Regardless of your career trajectory, the awareness of getting older will one day enter your thoughts. Most of us will probably work 40-50 years; this may seem like a long stretch to a 20-year-old, but to someone in her late 30's or early 40's, the reality of the finite nature of life includes the realization of the limited time she has to make all her career dreams come true.

The age at which a mid-life crisis strikes a person is fairly consistent with his health and general contentment. Healthy and happy people may have a later crisis, as they have fewer major challenges facing them as they age. But each person will eventually have to admit that their life has a beginning and an end point; all that humans do will become dust. That's a sobering thought.

For the person who's had a great career, the crisis might surface as a yearning to do all those things that were pushed aside in youth. The engineer wants to explore her artistic side; the teacher wants to be a student. Hobbies and volunteer activities are possible outlets for these yearnings, but for some, they are not enough. Only a full-fledged change will do.

The good news is that all the career exercises in this book are equally useful at all stages of life. Finding out about a previously undeveloped part of yourself is as exciting when you're old as when you're young.

For those whose previous careers are cut short due to their being fired, laid off, or no longer being physically or mentally able to function in those careers, the good news is exactly the same as above. Once any self-pity, resentment, or panic have been dealt with, you are ready to explore a new career which may be even more fulfilling than your past jobs, as it may incorporate the skills, abilities, and values you've gained from maturity. As had been the case throughout your career, you may find encouragement, advice, and recommendations from your previous professional experiences and your relationships with colleagues, former bosses, and customers.

Retirement or re-careering?

In the 21st century, the nature and the very definition of "retirement" are changing. As people live longer and enjoy better health than their parents and grandparents, the notion of stopping work completely at a particular age is being questioned on several levels. Not only must you have very significant financial resources to live 20 or 30 years after official retirement (whether or not you have a part-time job, work as a consultant, or start your own business), you must also have a continuing purpose in life to be happy and healthy.

Retiring with plenty of money, great health, and absorbing hobbies is a cultural ideal that is starting to show its weakness. As a goal, this view of retirement seems to provide an outstanding incentive for very hard work, thrift, careful self-monitoring of overall health, and development of an avocation during your prime years of life (ages 25-65). For the generation that retired in the 1980s and 1990s, this incentive made sense and paid off nicely for those with jobs that carried excellent pension plans and solid healthcare benefits.

In the 21st century, those jobs are slipping away. Many of the corporations that formed the bedrock of the US economy have been hit hard by global competition, financial incompetence, or fraud, meaning that pensions may not be available to retirees. And even for those whose believe that their investments and pensions are dependable, what is there to do with all that free time? A lifetime of working 60-80-hour weeks comes to an abrupt halt, to be followed by complete idleness. For the person who didn't have time to prepare a post-retirement life plan, this is a chilling change. Used to being in charge of dozens, hundreds, or thousands of employees, the new retiree finds herself in charge of walking the dog. This is a letdown, to say the least.

Keeping one foot in the world of work by easing from full-time to part-time in your job is one possibility; working as a consultant or even volunteering, perhaps with the Peace Corps or similar organization, is another way to use your hard-won knowledge and skills in your career field. Starting your own business, while requiring a prodigious outlay of energy and money, is another option.

Don't let your career define who you are or consume your life; you are much more than your job

In the midst of building and sustaining your career, don't overlook building and sustaining a personal life. Your family, children, friends, fellow hobby enthusiasts, members of your religious community, colleagues from professional associations, and acquaintances from national and international travel form your personal networks. These relationships have sustained you through your life and are just as important as the career in which you earn your living. If you have this kind of personal support system, a time of employment transition will be far easier to manage.

Professional networking groups are a good source of colleagues who can help you manage your career by giving you feedback on your current job's relative good and bad points and providing job leads for career advancement. These groups may offer continuing education opportunities and chances to increase your leadership skills by holding an office or working on a committee. Although attending a professional association meeting may seem like more "work," it's really a time to compare yourself to your professional colleagues and assess your career strengths and weaknesses.

Settling into your new job may require tremendous energy and attention, but thinking beyond your new assignment to what may come next is even more difficult. Yet it's only by staying ahead of the game that you can prepare yourself for all the changes to come in your career. You may be able to stay snug in one organization for many years, especially if you work for the federal or a state government, but even such safe havens are not what they once were. Budget cuts, government shutdowns, lack of sufficient customers, inability to compete due to inefficient practices and outdated equipment, and rapid political change have made all organizations vulnerable. The best philosophy is to never stop being in charge of your career.

. . . .

Steps to Reinventing Your Future

1. Is professional networking just for hard-core business types, or do you need to activate your networks for every kind of job?

2. How can you be a responsible and cooperative member of all the networks you belong to? Give three specific ways you can be a contributing member.

3. Why do people sometimes feel burned by members of their network? Have you ever felt that someone in one of your networks did not treat you with professional courtesy?

4. What are symptoms that you and your job are no longer a good match?

5. How can you plan your long-term career, considering unexpected changes, brand-new opportunities, and your post-retirement life?

Chapter Seven: Work in the future: what will change?

The workforce of the future is likely to consist mostly of those fortunate individuals who have decided to become unstoppable learning machines and who have their eyes open to find a need and fill it. All the knowledge, experience, education, and skills that workers have gained up until now will not be enough in the years ahead. Radical reshaping of the workplace is already upon us, and these reshaping forces will become stronger and more disruptive of "business as usual."

The people who will thrive in the future will be curious, generous, and open-minded. Their flexibility and interest in what's new will be the key to their career paths as they work in a world that's being changed by four dominant areas of change: advancements in technology, the interconnected global economy, climate change, and new attitudes and expectations about work. Critical thinking and problem-solving skills will be essential for all successful people as we are confronted with more complex and interconnected challenges.

The impact of ever-emerging new technologies

Anyone who was alive before the 21st century has already lived through enormous technological change. Technology has completely reshaped every industry including business, scientific fields, communications, healthcare, education, engineering, and the arts. Obvious changes involve IT (information technology) that permeates every office, classroom, and laboratory with software and hardware that make quick work of most daily routine tasks.

Humans have been writing extensively about these technological advances since the Industrial Revolution of the 1800s. The self-cleaning house, self-driving car, and robot maid dreams of the 1960s have come true, and then some. Human Resources, for example, no longer has to hire people to train employees; videos and self-paced programs do it faster and cheaper. Robots make phone calls to remind you about your upcoming doctor's appointment or to tell you a bill is due; robots answer the phone and route your calls to your cable provider several times before allowing you to speak to a person. Apps to pay your bills, turn on your lawn sprinklers, and apply for jobs are commonplace. It seems that many things a person can do, an intelligent machine can do.

What's more, technology can diagnose illnesses, auto-pilot jets, rain down explosives from drones a mile high, hand out tickets for people who run red lights, and manage the US federal government payroll. Nearly everyone has a smartphone, tablet, or laptop, giving them access to anyone by email and Skype. Instagram and Twitter let people share photos of their dinner or sound off on whatever bothers them at the moment. '

These instant communications allow everyone to connect to the greater culture and have a voice. Connecting with our peers lets us get a big picture of our employer, our industry, and our place in the world. People can share ideas, insights, and attitudes laterally rather than waiting for all information to come down from above in the form of distant, remote dictates of top management. Change happens person-to-person, easily and efficiently.

Most of these technological advances seem good. But what is gained in one place is often lost in another. The old-fashioned office manager who could solve any problem is being replaced by a string of low-wage temporary workers who don't get health insurance, a 401K, or paid holidays. These temps can't know the history, culture, and cherished attributes that have made the company what it is—

they only know what happened today. Brick-and-mortar bookshops, craft stores, and movie theaters are pushed out of business by online versions. The jobs in those physical places are lost or parceled into tiny tasks that can be automated. It's not that clerks from bookstores start to work online when their store closes; their jobs simply vanish as computers take over.

Naturally, employers welcome new technologies that substitute software for people. The cost savings are significant, and the tiring necessity of getting along with people in the workplace is diminished. Telecommuting, job sharing, temps, and every kind of contingent employment result in transient, task-based relationships rather than solid, long-lasting groups of colleagues and employers. On the surface, this is efficient, but what does this lack of continuity and mutual commitment do to institutions in the long run?

The workers of the next decades will deal with an entirely different employer/employee relationship. Without the comforts of knowing your job and your employer in a meaningful and predictable way, you will be dependent on your own ability to match your skills, experience, and open-minded attitude to the needs you see around you. Everyone will become, in effect, a self-employed consultant who proves his or her value in each new assignment. Job security based on longevity, tenure, or good performance in the past will be less and less significant in career success.

With new technology comes constant change. No sooner is a policy or procedure implemented than it's already outdated. People who relish this kind of fluidity, who can thrive in uncertainty and perpetual questioning of the most efficient and effective ways to fulfill an organization's key mission, will be in high demand in the years to come.

The impact of the world economy

Simply keeping up with world news is enough to demonstrate the dramatic ways in which the economic performance of one country can affect the whole planet. Government graft or instability, the volatility of the stock market, immigration and emigration, climate change, wars, unforeseeable shifts in consumer demand, weather catastrophes, epidemics, and just plain bad luck in one place reverberates everywhere. Clearly, the global economy is upon us.

The world can seem chaotic, clueless, and perplexed to a frightening degree. If you consider how countries are interwoven by financial investments, business transactions, educational exchanges, political alliances, medical research, artistic innovations, journalistic connections, and immigration, it becomes clear that no one is unaffected by what happens far away.

The economy of the coming decades will, in all likelihood, be even more interconnected. Although one response to globalization is an inward, self-protective instinct that can turn into isolationism and nationalism, the nationalistic platforms that may get politicians elected will fail to slow down the expansion of the global marketplace. Actually withdrawing from the global economy in order to put "my country" first is impossible. We've seen such former isolationists as China move away from its socialist planned economy to become a key player in international business, using a quasi-capitalist model in which business must expand to succeed. Expansion comes only when businesses and organizations provide products and services that people will buy and use. State planning from the top down, meant to restrict consumers to whatever that country can produce, will not work when people can easily observe the technological and material advances all around them.

What this means to those of us who want to prepare for the workplace of the future is simple: constant, rapid, and pervasive change. As we noted in Chapter Five on working abroad, having well-developed skills for a particular kind of job is merely the basic requirement for finding interesting and rewarding employment when you are competing with people from all over the world. What you will need to add to your repertoire of education, skills, expertise, and knowledge are the following qualities:

- Sincere appreciation for diversity in the workplace;

- Respect for values and attitudes very different from your own;

- Flexibility to do things in new ways without clinging to the tried-and-true;

- Willingness to learn something new and different every day;

- Realization that keeping your skills sharp and up-to-date is your own responsibility;

- Gratitude towards the many people who've helped you and strong desire to help others in the same way;

- The firm determination to take charge of your career.

In all the discussions about staying competitive in global markets, finding customers for business expansion, using resources wisely, and positioning an organization to take advantage of emerging opportunities, it's easy to lose sight of some eternal verities. The successful worker of the future will add to these considerations some of the intangibles of work: the basic human desires for autonomy, meaning, authenticity, and integrity. While no one expects a job to provide opportunities to fulfill all these desires, it's true that work can be more than just skills and tasks. The job-seeker of the future may be willing to trade a high salary for the chance to work creatively and according to their own strengths.

Increasingly, as the highly-competitive and ever-changing global marketplace threatens to pull apart the people who work in it, there will be a strong need for creating an entirely new kind of work environment that will build community. When the workplace is fragmented in the name of efficiency and productivity, people lose some of what is valuable and crucial for personal happiness: the knowledge that they are part of something bigger than their own individual selves, the feeling that their contributions are vital and appreciated, and the satisfaction of making friends and developing teams. If employers don't provide this sense of belonging and community, smart workers will do it themselves. They will look for opportunities to contribute to the common good and to make the institutions around them more humane, more responsive to human capabilities and needs, and better adapted to the changing circumstances that are a result of the impact of the global economy.

The impact of impending climate change

As catastrophic weather and higher sea levels due to melting of polar ice caps become more and more disruptive around the world, increasing numbers of people will search for new homes and jobs. It's estimated that hundreds of millions will be affected by climate change in the 21st century; these climate refugees may outnumber the political and economic refugees who created a humanitarian crisis in Europe in the 2010s.

Given the response to those political and economic refugees (who in the 2010s became known as illegal immigrants as they fled political and social turmoil in the Middle East, Africa, and South and Central America), it seems likely that climate refugees will not be welcome unless they bring with them the means to support themselves. You could imagine two scenarios that might emerge from such an enormous movement of people and resources around the globe: new business opportunities as capital flows and skilled people start businesses, or political and economic chaos as countries close their borders and reject refugees. Nationalistic political and economic policies of the 2010s are one reaction to such massive change: countries want to make themselves into self-sufficient fortresses and keep newcomers out. But in an era when technology and deep international networks are tying people together, trying to go it alone as a nation will not work.

What does this mean for people looking for jobs? One natural conclusion is that the environmental sector will be desperate for people to help mitigate the effects of climate change. A rich new vein of jobs and entrepreneurial opportunities will be available for anyone with the education, skills, experience, and interest to manage and slow down these tremendous forces that we are only beginning to understand. So far, humans have been able to adjust to structural changes in natural resources and social relationships; we have confidence that smart people who care about the viability of our planet as a place to live will be able to implement innovative strategies to adapt to change while trying to control its spread. At the same time, the world will need every bit of imagination, compassion for others, generosity, and celebration of human life that we can muster. Each person has the potential to make a meaningful and valuable contribution to the fate of the planet in this time of global interconnectedness.

New attitudes and expectations about work

Along with the impact of new technology, the interconnected world economy, and climate change, the workplace will be reimagined by the workers themselves. Far from seeing themselves as passive pawns that can be rearranged at the whim of the organizations where they work, these employees are empowered to be the architects of their own future.

With the elimination of job security caused in part by the "vulture capitalism" of the 2010s, creative people are waking up to the fact that they must be aware of and make full use of all their professional opportunities. During the 2007-2009 US Recession, companies and organizations eliminated many thousands of jobs in an effort to cut costs and stay solvent. But after the recession officially ended, the jobs did not return. Instead, the business model went from the "lean and mean" philosophy of the 1980s and 1990s to the vulture capitalist mode of making a profit from the misfortune of others (companies that were underperforming or going out of business). Maybe there's nothing morally wrong with making money that way, but the attitude of exploiting the weak has led to a job market where no employee can count on keeping a job when times get rough. Rather than trimming other costs (such as their own executive salaries) when profits are down, many businesses and organizations now operate on the principle of jettisoning employees at the first sign of trouble. They may rehire them, but how can people live in the meantime? And who wants to work in such an atmosphere of alienation and uncertainty?

Although the vulture capitalist approach to business was not intended to spark employee independence, that has been the result. Rather than expect their employers to treat them well (to include them in discussions during times of crisis and to make financial sacrifices to keep good employees working), perceptive people are taking their futures into their own hands. Their efforts are bearing fruit in important ways:

- The development of new approaches to meaningful workplace and social interaction;

- Promoting practices that stress content over form, depth over shallowness, and truth over convenient fiction or make-believe;

- Adoption of a new business and civic model built on the shared understanding that greed is robbing our own children and grandchildren of a sustainable future;

- An acceptance of the reality that no one can count on keeping a job for life and that everyone must be constantly aware of the forces of technological transformation, global competition, and climate change.

People who thrive in the middle of turbulent change see themselves as in charge of their destiny. They are the CEOs and Presidents of their careers, seeking to achieve the goals they have assigned themselves. Although they may suffer setbacks due to decisions made without sufficient information (or just bad luck), they are resilient and will spring back. They will continue to look for and create career opportunities that fulfill the basic human desires for autonomy, meaning, authenticity, and integrity.

In addition, these strong and self-motivated people will require of employers that their working environments be stimulating, fair, safe, and motivating. They will not settle for anything less than a workplace where the achievements of everyone involved are acknowledged and celebrated. In these work settings, workers can contribute something worthwhile and honorable, with a lasting impact on society. For all this to happen, the principles and practices of vulture capitalism will need to give way to morals and ethics that recognize the worth and value of every person. Technology will be the servant of the workforce, allowing people to work fewer hours as software takes over many routine tasks without eliminating the parts of a job that require human effort: building and maintaining trust, applauding innovation, and working in team settings to maximize intellectual input.

During the next decades of the 21st century, workers will be perpetually self-employed, always scanning the horizon for golden opportunities. Successful workers will be part of a living network of friends, family, colleagues, college classmates, former bosses, and friends of friends who contribute job leads and introductions that advance each other's careers. Each job becomes a new consulting assignment, adding to people's value in the network and giving them the chance to develop new skills, take pertinent classes, and expand their repertoire as professionals.

This kind of self-selected contingent work does not create insecurity; instead, it will be a major factor in restructuring the culture of the workplace. As the changes keep happening in technology, the global economy, and the earth's climate, both workers and the organizations where they work will keep adjusting. Some will get ahead of the change; others will run to catch up. You can decide, right now, to accept the challenge of working in the 21st century. Claim your own future. Use everything you have to craft a career you can enjoy, where you contribute as much as you receive and where you can find the meaning and satisfaction of reconciling your goals with your work. This is what it means to reinvent your future.

. . . .

Steps to Reinventing Your Future

1. How is technology changing the career landscape in your chosen industry?

2. Further education in technology may seem like a good way to upgrade your skills, but consider that education usually follows rather than leads in innovation. How can you access the truly innovative minds and research in your industry?

3. How does on-going climate change influence your life?

Afterword: You have what it takes to succeed

Unquestionably, finding a job that fits you, in a place where you fit, is a huge challenge when the job market is so vast and turbulent. Your future work place is not likely to be an oasis of stability, job security, and tranquility. But we are confident that you can equip yourself with all you need to build a satisfying and productive career if you use the methods and strategies we have provided in a systematic and thoughtful way. It's up to you to take charge of your career, using all your skills and abilities to reinvent your own future and to help the people around you to do the same.

As you make your way through life, please keep in mind that you will never really finish reinventing your future. The biggest challenges in today's job market are the speed and unpredictability with which it changes. But for the person who has done the hard work of self-analysis, job exploration, interviewing with many organizations, keeping in touch with professional colleagues, and being aware of the shifting winds of social change, this speed and unpredictability offer exciting golden opportunities.

We wish you well on the life-long adventure of reinventing your future!

Jaroslav and Sara Tusek

March 20, 2019

Resources and Recommended Reading

Books

Bolles, Richard. *What Color Is Your Parachute? 2019: A Practical Manual for Job-Hunters and Career-Changers.* Ten Speed Press, 2018. The best-known classic—the first popular comprehensive career development book that helps people match their interests, values, and skills with appropriate jobs. Written in a light-hearted tone.

Burnett, Bill and Dave Evans. *Designing Your Life.* Knopf, 2016. "The prototype for a happy life…Burnett and Evans show how to apply Stanford's famous design principles to finding your place in the world, as a recent graduate or mid-career."—NPR's Brian Lehrer

Encyclopedia of Careers and Vocational Guidance. 17th Edition, Chicago, Ill: Ferguson Publishing Co., 2017.
This set of books includes entries for many careers with information such as the history of the profession, job duties, education and experience requirements, expected earnings, and job outlook. There is also a Career Guidance section to help you chose a career, write a resume and cover letter, and interview successfully. This is an expensive set of books that should be available in a public or university library.

Farr, J.M. & L. Shatkin. *50 Best Jobs for Your Personality.* St. Paul, MN, JIST Publishing, 2012. Based on John Holland's widely accepted theory of vocational personalities, this book elaborates on proven research that matches personality to a career that brings work satisfaction and success.

Figler, Howard. *The Complete Job Search Handbook.* Holt Paperbacks, 2013. This classic manual takes you from self-analysis to the job search.

Graeber, David. *Bullshit Jobs: A Theory*. Simon & Schuster, 2018. Does every job perform a vital service? Graeber provides entertaining stories and intriguing questions about the value of work.

Griffith, Susan. *Work Your Way Around the World*. Crimson Publishing, 2017. As the title suggests, you can combine a love of adventure with getting a job. Examples include teaching English or working in an environmental organization.

Guinness, Os. *The Call: Finding and Fulfilling the Central Purpose of Your Life*. Thomas Nelson, 2018. A serious look at the Christian idea of vocation or calling.

Henderson, Carter. *Free Enterprise Moves East: Doing Business from Prague to Vladivostok*. Ics Pr, 1996. Business executives from post-soviet countries adapt to the free market. International Leadership Institute program graduates are interviewed.

Irish, Richard, *Go Hire Yourself an Employer*. Knopf Doubleday Publishing Group, 1973. An older book but still relevant. Irish changes your perspective from job seeker to job chooser.

Krannich, Ron. *Change your Job, Change your Life*. Impact Publications, 9th edition, 2004. A classic career development book with practical tips on combining your work with your life's goals.

McMillon, Bill, et al. *Volunteer Vacations: Short-Term Adventures That Will Benefit You and Others*. Chicago Review Press, Chicago, IL, 2012. Working as a committed volunteer in a cause that matters to you is a valuable way to explore careers of interest.

Medley, H. Anthony. *Sweaty Palms: The Neglected Art of Being Interviewed*. Amazon Digital Services LLC, 2011. Includes hundreds of sample interview questions and answers.

Michelozzi, Betty. *Coming Alive from Nine to Five*. McGraw-Hill, 2003. Michelozzi is strong on the values clarification and personal growth aspects of career development.

Occupational Outlook Quarterly. Washington, DC: U.S. Department of Labor, Bureau of Labor Statistics.
This journal supplements and updates the information in the Occupational Outlook Handbook. Each issue includes articles about various careers. Most public and university libraries will carry this book. You can access much of this information online at www.bls.gov/ooh/.

Reich, Robert. *The Common Good*. Knopf, 2018. Reich, who served under three US presidents as an advisor in public and economic policy, makes a strong case for factoring in the needs of an entire society when making personal decisions. This book offers a deeper understanding of how networks operate in the real world.

Seligson, Hannah. *Mission: Adulthood: How the 20-Somethings of Today Are Transforming Work, Love, and Life*. Diversion Books, 2014. Seligson, a writer for the *New York Times*, follows the lives of seven members of "Gen Y" and how they experience the relationship of their careers to the rest of their lives.

Sher, Barbara. *Wishcraft*. Ballantine Books; 2nd edition, 2003. The classic book for dreamers and for making dreams come true.

Tokumitsu, Miya. *Do What You Love: And Other Lies about Success and Happiness*. Regan Arts, 2015. The author argues that the idea of work as a passion and a means of self-realization can be used by employers to manipulate employers into accepting unfair pay and working conditions. For job-seekers, this argument provides confidence as they interview and a perspective to help them negotiate a better deal when they accept a job offer.

Tusek, Sara D. & Jaroslav B. *21st Century Jobs.* International Leadership Institute Publications, Lake Mary, FL, 2009. Comprehensive career development manual that offers help to job-seekers who want to find the jobs they can like and do best.

Veruki, Peter. *The 250 Job Interview Questions you'll most likely get asked . . . and the answers that will get you hired!* Adams Media Corporation, 1999. Former Fortune 500 recruiter and Vanderbilt University business school placement director Peter Veruki gives insightful commentary on common interview questions.

Websites

The United States Labor Department, Bureau of Labor Statistics maintains a website where you can get facts and figures about thousands of jobs. On this website, you can use the digital version of the Occupational Outlook Handbook to get job descriptions, salary ranges, and other pertinent information. You can buy your own copy or go to the Reference Section of any large public library and use the book there. www.bls.gov/ooh/.

University and college career services offices have a wealth of information online, free to the public. Online job-posting boards, aptitude tests, interest inventories, and personality tests are on many of these websites and can help point you in a direction if you are just beginning your job search. Go to the website for your alma mater or favorite university and find the career services pages. If you are a graduate of a college, you may be able to get some help from Career Services: counseling, resume development, and job leads are all typically found in Career Services.

Websites for help-wanted ads are easy to find on the world-wide web. The largest ones get the most publicity, have the most jobs, and attract the most job hunters. Therefore, bear in mind that you are just one of hundreds of people applying for any given job. A better route is a specialized job board to a site run by a professional organization (for example, *The Chronicle of Higher Education* website for jobs in colleges and universities). As in any on-line job search, looking at .org and .edu sites, which tend to be less commercial and more focused, is better than using only .coms, which tend to be all things to all people, resulting in your casting your job-search net into too wide a sea.

Appendix: Examples for Chapter Two

"What I Believe and Why": The America I Believe In by Colin Powell *As heard on NPR's Morning Edition, April 11, 2005.*

Colin Powell spent 35 years in the military, rising from ROTC in college to become a four-star general and Chairman of the Joint Chiefs of Staff during the first Gulf War. He has worked in the administrations of six Presidents including serving as Secretary of State from 2001 – 2005.

I believe in America and I believe in our people.

Later this month, I will be participating in a ceremony at Ellis Island where I will receive copies of the ship manifest and the immigration documents that record the arrival in America of my mother, Maud Ariel McKoy, from Jamaica aboard the motor ship Turialba in 1923. My father, Luther Powell, had arrived three years earlier at the Port of Philadelphia.

They met in New York City, married, became Americans and raised a family. By their hard work and their love for this country, they enriched this nation and helped it grow and thrive. They instilled in their children and grandchildren that same love of country and a spirit of optimism.

My family's story is a common one that has been told by millions of Americans. We are a land of immigrants: A nation that has been touched by every nation and we, in turn, touch every nation. And we are touched not just by immigrants but by the visitors who come to America and return home to tell of their experiences. I believe that our greatest strength in dealing with the world is the openness of our society and the welcoming nature of our people. A good stay in our country is the best public diplomacy tool we have.

After 9/11 we realized that our country's openness was also its vulnerability. We needed to protect ourselves by knowing who was coming into the country, for what purpose and to know when they left. This was entirely appropriate and reasonable. Unfortunately, to many foreigners we gave the impression that we were no longer a welcoming nation. They started to go to schools and hospitals in other countries, and frankly, they started to take their business elsewhere. We can't allow that to happen. Our attitude has to be, we are glad you are here. We must be careful, but we must not be afraid.

As I traveled the world as secretary of state, I encountered anti-American sentiment. But I also encountered an underlying respect and affection for America. People still want to come here.

Refugees who have no home at all know that America is their land of dreams. Even with added scrutiny, people line up at our embassies to apply to come here.

You see, I believe that the America of 2005 is the same America that brought Maud Ariel McKoy and Luther Powell to these shores, and so many millions of others. An America that each day gives new immigrants the same gift that my parents received. An America that lives by a Constitution that inspires freedom and democracy around the world. An America with a big, open, charitable heart that reaches out to people in need around the world. An America that sometimes seems confused and is always noisy. That noise has a name, it's called democracy and we use it to work through our confusion.

An America that is still the beacon of light to the darkest corner of the world.

Last year I met with a group of Brazilian exchange students who had spent a few weeks in America. I asked them to tell me about their experience here. One young girl told me about the night the 12 students went to a fast food restaurant in Chicago. They ate and then realized they did not have enough money to pay the bill. They were way short. Frightened, they finally told the waitress of their problem. She went away and she came back in a little while saying, "I talked to the manager and he said, 'It's ok.'" The students were still concerned because they thought the waitress might have to pay for it out of her salary. She smiled and she said, "No, the manager said he is glad you are here in the United States. He hopes you are having a good time, he hopes you are learning all about us. He said it's on him."

It is a story that those young Brazilian kids have told over and over about America. That's the America I believe in, that's the America the world wants to believe in.

Independently produced for NPR by Jay Allison and Dan Gediman with John Gregory and Viki Merrick. Edited by Ellen Silva.
Sample essay from This I Believe: This I Believe is a national media project engaging people in writing, sharing, and discussing the core values and beliefs that guide their daily lives. From http://www.thisibelieve.org/aboutus.html

Appendix: Examples for Chapter Two

Write-your-own obituary exercise: This is a fictional

   example.

March 13, 2015: "Congresswoman Kline dies; Detroit Community

Leader for more than Seventy Years"

Dorothy Jenkins Kline, long-time political activist and member of the

United States House of Representatives, died yesterday in her home

in Dearborn Heights following a brief illness. She was 98 years old.

   Born in Detroit on November 12, 1916, Kline was raised by

her grandmother after her mother died of pneumonia in 1919. She

never knew her father. Kline's grandmother, Arletta Jenkins, was

well-known in her neighborhood for helping anyone in need; as a

time when African Americans had few financial resources and were

often devastated by the death of the family breadwinner, Mrs. Jenkins

started a local life insurance company that collected a small amount

of money each week from hard-working African American who

wanted to provide some financial security for their families. This

modest company grew into American Life, which is today the leading

provider of life insurance in Michigan and the surrounding states.

Congresswoman Kline benefited from her grandmother's example of practical compassion. A serious student, in high school Kline began to develop a reputation as a hard worker who "got things done." At Detroit's West Street High, Kline was valedictorian; she established the Young Democrats Club, which supported local candidates and provided tutoring for low-income children. Kline was awarded a full-tuition scholarship to Detroit College, a small Catholic women's college noted for its academic excellence. There she continued to develop her two life-long interests, politics and education. She was elected Class President every year she attended Detroit College, and attended seminars in government leadership at Michigan State University. While in college, Kline created the Detroit Community Coalition, an advocacy group that lobbied politicians on neighborhood improvement issues while delivering service to poor children through free-meal programs, tutoring, and foster care services. The Great Depression had made life very perilous for people already poor, and Kline was determined to unite the community to help itself.

Upon graduation from Detroit College, Kline took a job teaching in her alma mater, West Street High. She was appalled to find the students still using the same out-of-date textbooks she had used and began her campaign to change the unfair budget allocation process in the city school district; this process discriminated against the poor and African American schools. Her vocal support of the poorest schools and neighborhood caught the attention of the status-quo conservative city political machine, which approached her with an offer of a new teaching position in the most prestigious, well-funded city high school in exchange for her support. Kline refused this offer, and thus began her political career.

Kline was elected in 1942 as a city ward representative for her own ward, becoming an influential City Council member known for her courage and honesty. When WWII ended, Kline introduced legislation to receive returning veterans with job services, housing options, and educational opportunities in Detroit. The Detroit Community Coalition, which administered charitable monies from this legislation, became a national example of a grass-roots political organization as a powerful agent of social change.

To become more effective in her political work, Kline determined to attend law school. In a fateful decision, Kline accepted Brandeis University's School of Law offer and moved to metropolitan Boston. Here she met her future husband and life

partner, Arthur Kline. Graduating summa sum laude, Mrs. Kline had

several offers in well-known Boston law firms, perhaps eager to show

their liberal politics by hiring an African American. Both she and her

husband decided, though, to make their home in Detroit.

The 1950's and 1960's were a time of great change for

African Americans. Through churches, schools and neighborhood

organizations such as the Detroit Community Coalition, African

Americans began to act as a unified force to eradicate

institutionalized racism. Kline and her husband became leaders in the

Detroit civil rights movement, inviting the Reverend Dr. Martin

Luther King, Jr. and the Reverend Jesse Jackson to help organize civil

rights demonstrations. In 1969 Kline was elected Deputy Mayor of

Detroit; she was tapped to serve on state and national committees

seeking solutions for the troubled inner cities of the United States in

an effort to stem racial conflict and bring peace to riot-torn

neighborhoods in the wake of the assassination of Dr. King in 1968.

Deputy Mayor Kline, along with her husband Arthur, a

professor of law at the University of Michigan-Detroit, became well-

known as they worked to end the economic and social inequality that fueled the anger of young African Americans. In 1974, Kline was persuaded to run for Congress, becoming a Democratic member of the United States House of Representatives for the 3rd District of Michigan, including Detroit and parts of six surrounding counties.

For the next 20 years, Congresswoman Kline served her district with competence and vigor. She was appointed to the House Committee on Ways and Means (subcommittee on Income Security and Family Support); the House Committee for Education and Labor (subcommittee on Early Childhood, Elementary and Secondary Education; subcommittee on Healthy Families and Communities); and the Select Presidential Committee for Community Development. Kline co-authored (with her husband) the Stafford Commission Report on Early Childhood Poverty in the United States.

Congresswoman Kline retired in 1984. She is survived by her husband Arthur; her daughters Cherie and Monica; her grandsons Devon and Patrick and her granddaughters Olivia and April. The funeral will be on March 17 at 2 pm at Gracious Savior Church in Detroit.

About the International Leadership Institute (ILI)

WHO WE ARE

Founded in 1985 in Princeton, NJ, we are a private international business, based in Florida and Prague, Czech Republic. We specialize in designing and delivering leadership and career development programs (*Business Leadership Forum: USA*, *Reinventing Your Future* seminars); English language skills-building programs (*American English Language Institute*) and *Travel-and-Learn* Programs for European and American participants in the United States and in Europe.

Since 1991, the Institute has worked with more than 15,000 individuals in career development, language-building, and executive education programs. Our program participants are from Bosnia & Herzegovina, Bulgaria, China, Croatia, the Czech Republic, Germany, Japan, Lithuania, Macedonia, Romania, Slovakia, South Korea, Switzerland, Ukraine, and the United States.

International Leadership Institute Publications is a publisher of books, reports, and periodicals aimed at inspiring and assisting people in three key areas: seeking understanding of contemporary leadership challenges and methods, building more effective career and communication skills, and improving American English language skills.

WHAT WE DO

Reinventing Your Future Seminars and Workshops

These ILI seminars offer a systematic and strategic approach to matching your career-related assets and qualifications to the needs of organizations and businesses. The biggest changes today are the speed and unpredictability with which the labor market changes. The person who has done the hard work of self-analysis, job exploration, interviewing with many organizations, keeping in touch with professional colleagues, and being aware of the shifting winds of social change is equipped to spot and act on exciting job-related opportunities. Seminars are offered to the general public as platforms for exchanging information and discerning career-related interests and trends. Workshops are offered for job-changers in both group and individual settings and focus on job-search strategies; typical workshop programs last 4 weeks.

American English Language Institute

Our goal is to assist individuals and groups of people so that they gain skills in reading, writing, and listening. Each program is tailored to the particular level of skill and needs of the participants. For example, *American English Language Immersion Programs* bring young European participants to the U. S. for program lasting 3 weeks to two months. In these programs, student participants live with an American host family, in college dorms, or on the road, improving their English language skills by using English as their main means of communication. Programs include educational, social, cultural, religious, and recreational activities to allow participants a chance to develop a rich and wide vocabulary in English, gain an understanding of key American values, and become fluent in English through substantive conversations with native speakers. Programs in Europe focus on skill development, cultural understanding, and the ability to function effectively in environments where English is spoken and written.

Travel-and-Learn Programs in the United States and in Europe

Travel with a twist: more than mere tourism, travel-and-learn programs introduce participants to the people, culture, geography, political and economic systems, and history of the countries visited. The Institute has a deep commitment to bringing people together through mutual understanding; these programs give participants the chance to see beyond the typical tourist sites and begin to develop an on-going relationship with the people and countries visited.

Business Leadership Forum: USA (BLF) training programs are delivered in the United States. From 1990 to 2006, ILI offered these executive education programs on a regular basis, with notable results. Over US$1 billion in international business activities was generated by *BLF* executive education program participants in that time period.

Programs include some or all of the following business/educational activities:

- Scheduled business meetings in the companies of potential business partners;

- Graduate university seminars on business topics; English language tune-up courses;

- Scheduled appointments with executives interested in exploring mutually-beneficial forms of cooperation, including business opportunities;

- On-site visits and tours; internships and job shadowing;

- Participation in trade shows, professional association meetings, and conferences; networking functions, including Chamber of Commerce mixers and panels;

- Social, cultural, and recreational activities that help them experience the American way of life.

BLF executive participant profile:

- From Bulgaria, Croatia, the Czech Republic, Lithuania, Macedonia, Romania, Slovakia and the Ukraine, and ranging in age from 22 to over 60;

- Representing a variety of professions and industries: machine design and production; journalism, computer systems and parts; product distribution and logistics; government ministry of transportation; civic reform; financial services; banking; insurance; stock market; pension funds; aircraft production; import/export; the law; higher education; and software development, to name a few.

We've worked with US-based businesses, agencies, and non-profit organizations to deliver the *BLF* and similar programs. Major partners and affiliates include the following:

- The United States Department of State Agency for International Development *AID*, through the *World Learning/PTP-Europe*, *World Learning/TRANSIT* and *PIET* programs;

- Eleven Chambers of Commerce in Tennessee, Florida, the Czech Republic, and Slovakia;

- Fifteen government ministries and agencies in the Czech Republic, Slovakia, and the United States;

- 657 private businesses in twelve states and six countries:

- Eleven public and private universities in Tennessee, Georgia, Florida, Alabama, North Carolina, and the Czech Republic.

About us

ILI President & CEO Jaroslav Tusek has a five-decade career in which he has been deeply involved with leadership and career development. Jarda has written books and articles, taught graduate classes, and led executive education seminars and programs for individuals and groups, helping participants absorb key concepts and build their skills and abilities in both leadership and career development. He directed offices of career services at St. Lawrence University, New York Institute of Technology, and Covenant College and was co-founder and VP for Marketing at the Career Group in New York City. He directed the Operation Enterprise program at the American Management Association and served as program coordinator in several non-profit agencies.

ILI Managing Director Sara Tusek directed the career services office at The University of the South and served as career counselor at St Lawrence University. She has taught English and Writing to students from all over the world: the Caribbean; Central, South, and North America; Africa; Central and Eastern Europe; and East Asia. Sara has written books, articles, reports, and educational materials for international program participants. She holds a Master's

Degree in Education from Vanderbilt University and has extensive

experience in sociological and historical research, curriculum

development, and cross-cultural communications. Sara teaches

Writing at Seminole State College in Florida. She is the Executive

Editor of International Leadership Institute Publications, which

publishes books, manuals, fiction, educational and program materials,

and handbooks that support ILI's mission: "To promote and

facilitate leadership development activities that contribute to

sustaining a liberal democratic order promoting the common good,

building strong community ties, and encouraging individuals to act as

responsible citizens in their daily lives." Sara owns MRP, a consulting

firm offering publication and management services to businesses.

Jarda co-founded the International Leadership Institute in 1985

in Princeton, NJ. The firm's original mission was to train American

executives in the face of dramatically-increasing global competition in

manufacturing and financial services during the late 1980s. In this

work, Jarda drew on his international professional background. He

holds a Master's Degree in International Affairs from Columbia

University Graduate School of Public and International Affairs in

New York City and was awarded a postgraduate fellowship in international economics at the Institute of International Studies of the University of Geneva in Switzerland. There he worked as a consultant to the World Council of Churches. Jarda attended the Charles University School of Law Doctor of Jurisprudence program in Prague and the University of Oslo in Norway. Fluent in six languages (English, French, German, Czech, Russian and Norwegian), he is a long-time student of political, economic, social, and religious developments in East Central Europe.

In 1990, when communism collapsed in Czechoslovakia, Jarda and Sara returned to Jarda's native land to offer the Institute's services to the Czechoslovak Ministry of Industry and Trade. They developed programs to support the Czechoslovak economic and political transition from totalitarianism to freedom and democracy. ILI developed joint ventures from 1991 to 1997 with the Ministry of Industry and Trade of the Czech Republic, the Czech and Slovak Chambers of Commerce, the Jacksonville Chamber of Commerce, the World Trade Center-Chattanooga, Covenant College, the University of North Florida, and many other agencies, media outlets, businesses, and non-profit organizations for the delivery of the

Business Leadership Forum: USA programs which worked with more than 1,000 East and Central European business, government and professional leaders. From 1996—2006 the Institute served as a training organization for the United States Department of State in their AID (Agency for International Development) programs for East and Central European leaders; these programs were delivered via World Learning in Washington, DC. During more than 70 trips since 1991 to the Czech Republic, Slovakia, Hungary, Austria, Germany and Switzerland, Jarda and Sara have recruited participants for ILI programs and led groups of US educators, executives, students, and government leaders, helping them become more familiar with Central Europe.

Sara founded and directs the *American English Language Institute* to help people gain valuable skills in speaking, reading, and writing English. From 1990—2007, Sara provided language immersion programs in the United States for European students. During their US homestay, participants attended university classes, improved their English-speaking skills through daily interactions, received instruction in career development strategies, and developed their leadership abilities. From 2010-2013, ILI's main offices were in Prague, where

Sara ran programs for South Korean, Vietnamese, and Czech participants. Instruction focused on writing and reading skill development, as well as preparing for university admission. Back in the US, Sara works with international students to develop their ease and confidence in reading, writing, speaking, and listening to American English.

Jarda and Sara have extensive and varied international involvement in guiding people as they design careers in which they can thrive. *Reinventing Your Future* is their 10th book on this topic. Together, they have more than 70 years of experience in organizing, promoting and delivering career development workshops and individual counseling programs, working one-on-one and with small groups of clients from all over the world in a wide range of industries. Since 1990, their work together in the International Leadership Institute has been focused on leadership and career development programs, services, and publications that help program participants develop personal, educational, and career goals that will carry them through their lifetime. The Tuseks divide their time between Prague and Florida. They have two children, Noah and Melissa, a daughter-in-law, Tina, and a grandchild, Amelia.

www.ingramcontent.com/pod-product-compliance
Lightning Source LLC
Chambersburg PA
CBHW022059210326
41520CB00046B/625